Critical Reasoning & Philosophy

Critical Reasoning & Philosophy

A Concise Guide to Reading, Evaluating, and Writing Philosophical Works

Second Edition

M. Andrew Holowchak

ROWMAN & LITTLEFIELD PUBLISHERS, INC.
Lanham • Boulder • New York • Toronto • Plymouth, UK

Published by Rowman & Littlefield Publishers, Inc.
A wholly owned subsidiary of The Rowman & Littlefield Publishing Group, Inc.
4501 Forbes Boulevard, Suite 200, Lanham, Maryland 20706
http://www.rowmanlittlefield.com

Estover Road, Plymouth PL6 7PY, United Kingdom

British Library Cataloguing in Publication Information Available

Library of Congress Cataloging-in-Publication Data
Holowchak, Mark, 1958-
  Critical reasoning & philosophy : a concise guide to reading, evaluating & writing philosophical works / M. Andrew Holowchak. — 2nd ed.
      p. cm.
  Rev. ed. of: Critical reason and philosophy.
  Includes bibliographical references (p.   ).
  ISBN 978-1-4422-0521-5 (cloth : alk. paper) — ISBN 978-1-4422-0522-2 (pbk. : alk. paper) — ISBN 978-1-4422-0523-9 (electronic)
  1. Philosophy—Study and teaching. 2. Philosophy—Authorship. I. Holowchak, Mark, 1958- Critical reasoning and philosophy. II. Title. III. Title: Critical reasoning and philosophy.
  B52.H69 2011
  107.2—dc23   2011025445

♾™ The paper used in this publication meets the minimum requirements of American National Standard for Information Sciences—Permanence of Paper for Printed Library Materials, ANSI/NISO Z39.48-1992.

Printed in the United States of America

Contents

Preface   **vii**

Acknowledgments   **xiii**

PART I: INTRODUCTORY CONCERNS   **1**

Module 1   What Is Philosophy?   3

Module 2   Philosophy & Critical Reasoning   7

PART II: READING PHILOSOPHY   **11**

Module 3   General Form of a Philosophical Work   13

Module 4   Four Helpful Steps   19

PART III: EVALUATING PHILOSOPHY   **23**

Section A: Argument Recognition & Reconstruction   **25**

Module 5   Elements of Argument Recognition   27

Module 6   Standard Argument Form   35

Section B: Argument Evaluation   **43**

Module 7   Setting the Logical Boundaries   45

Module 8   Conditions of Acceptance & Rejection   51

Module 9   Three Common Deductive Arguments   55

Module 10   Common Inductive Arguments   61

Module 11   Common Fallacies   69

Section C: Reconstruction through Diagramming   **77**

Module 12   Fundamentals of Diagramming   79

Module 13   10 Diagrammatical Tips   85

PART IV: WRITING PHILOSOPHY   **93**

Section A: Preliminaries for Philosophical Essays   **95**

Module 14   13 General Tips for Writing   97

Module 15   Tips of Avoidance   101

Module 16   Common Mistakes   109

Section B: Writing Philosophical Essays   **117**

    Module 17   Preparing an Outline   119

    Module 18   Writing a Philosophical Thesis   123

    Module 19   Simple Critical Essay   127

    Module 20   Synthetic Critical Essay   131

Section C: Revising & Rewriting Philosophical Essays   **135**

    Module 21   Motivating a Rewrite   137

    Module 22   Suggestions for Revising and Rewriting Essays   139

APPENDICES   **141**

    Appendix A   Some Exercises for Diagramming   143

    Appendix B   Teacher/Student Comment Sheet   147

    Appendix C   Plan-for-Revision Sheet   149

Sources Cited   **151**

Preface

John Dewey said, "[I]t is no exaggeration to say that the measure of a civilization is the degree in which the method of cooperative intelligence replaces the method of brute conflict." This is a powerful and moving statement and one that is, I think, true. Civilization exists and flourishes, Dewey believes, only inasmuch as people adopt critical and cooperative attitudes toward solving problems.

The ancient Greek philosopher Socrates was perhaps the earliest thinker to recognize that point. Never claiming to know anything, Socrates spent most of his life in a cooperative search for truth, as he actively pursued knowledge with all who would search with him. In doing so, he fashioned a dialectical method of cooperative inquiry that is, in some form or another, increasingly used in classrooms across the globe today.

In the nineteenth century, John Stuart Mill in *On Liberty* championed a similar method in his search for answers to religious, moral, philosophical, and political questions. Mill stated:

> Truth, in the great practical concerns of life, is so much a question of the reconciling and combining of opposites that very few have minds sufficiently capacious and impartial to make the adjustment with an approach to correctness, and it has to be made by the rough process of a struggle between combatants fighting under hostile banners.

For any hope of success on unsettled issues, Mill believed that diversity of thought, the capacity for free expression of opinion, and an admission of fallibility by all involved were needed for progress. Any attempt to silence an opinion, he added, even one that was generally believed to be false, was an impediment to progress.

Prompted by the work of such pioneers and with local issues increasingly become global issues, today researchers are coming increasingly to see the value of using critical and cooperative models of learning in classrooms. Such models are of special importance in classes on philosophy, which, more than most other classes, challenge students to develop a critical attitude toward everyday-life issues.

Critical Reasoning & Philosophy: A Concise Guide to Reading, Evaluating, and Writing Philosophical Works, Ed. 2 is the culmination of numerous years of thinking about an integrative, cooperative, and critical approach to teaching introductory courses in philosophy. Philosophers in the analytic tradition are wedded to a specific type of analytic methodology that requires the honing and use of critical-reasoning skills. Students being introduced to philosophy need exposure to such skills and cannot fully appreciate philosophical analysis without them. Thus, students wishing to read, evaluate critically, and respond to a philosophical work must be able to recognize, reconstruct, and evaluate arguments and to express themselves philosophically in coherent and tightly argued essays that move philosophical debate forward.

With those ends in mind, I have created this text to complement introductory-level philosophy courses. It is especially suited for writing-intensive courses, in which students are asked to read primary-source materials and respond critically by putting forth and defending a philosophical thesis through thoughtful argumentation. Thus, this book is meant to complement introductory-level philosophy courses, where the focus in such courses is on learning how to do philosophy as much as it is on learning what certain philosophers think about certain issues.

As it aims to teach students how to read, evaluate, and write philosophy, the book begins analytically by giving students the tools and skills to recognize, break down, and analyze arguments before formally responding to them in writing. It ends synthetically by enabling students to advance and defend a philosophical position of their own in a synthetic critical essay.

Structure of *Critical Reasoning & Philosophy, Ed. 2*

The structure of the second edition of *Critical Reasoning & Philosophy* has changed to accommodate the express aims of the book more efficiently. Instead of six sections with 19 modules, it now comprises four parts—Introductory Concerns, Reading Philosophy, Evaluating Philosophy, and Writing Philosophy—and 22 modules.

Part I, Introductory Concerns, is a brief exposition of philosophy and critical thinking. Module 1 is a brief description of the nature of philosophy; Module 2 is a brief description of the relationship between critical reasoning and philosophy.

Part II, Reading Philosophy, contains two modules. The first aims to delineate the general structure of a well-formed philosophical work, whether of essay- or book-length. The second outlines four helpful steps for reading correctly that work. These were parts of one module in the first edition.

The third part, Evaluating Philosophy, contains three sections. Section A, Argument Recognition & Reconstruction, has two modules. The first marks out the elements of argument recognition. The second gives the guidelines for reconstructing arguments in what is commonly called "standard argument form." Section B, Argument Evaluation, comprises five modules. Module 7 sets up the logical boundaries of the meaning of statements by examining statement modality—i.e., necessary truths, necessary falsehoods, and contingent statements—as well as by examining what it means for two statements to be contradictory, inconsistent, consistent, and equivalent. Module 8 gives the conditions of accepting and rejecting arguments and a brief examination of the difference between inductive arguments, deductive arguments, and fallacies. Modules 9 and 10 list some of the most common inductive and deductive arguments. Finally, common fallacies are listed in Module 11. Section C concerns argument diagramming and is intended for instructors that wish to take things a bit further in the classroom. It has two modules. They explain the importance of diagramming for argument reconstruction, give the fundamentals of diagramming arguments, and offer 10 diagrammatical tips.

Part IV, Writing Philosophy, has three sections. Section A covers the preliminaries of writing a philosophical essay in three modules. While the first offers some general motivational tips for writing a good philosophical essay, the second offers some general writing tips for a good philosophical essay. The third is an elaboration of commonly made mistakes that students of philosophy especially will want to avoid. Section B concerns the writing of a philosophical essay. Module 17, which is new, describes the importance of an outline and explains how to write an outline to give a paper direction and keep it focused. Module 18 is about writing a philosophical thesis. Modules 19 and 20 describe the differences between what I call "simple critical essays" and "synthetic critical essays" and explain how to write each. Last, Section C contains two modules—one module in the first edition—which detail revising (Module 21) and rewriting (Module 22) philosophical essays.

The 22 modules of the second edition are complemented by three appendices. Appendix A offers some practice exercises from famous philosophers for argument diagramming. Appendices B and C complement the final section of Part IV on revising and rewriting philosophical essays. Appendix B is a sample comment sheet, to be filled out by the instructor or fellow students, for revising papers. Appendix C is a plan-for-revision sheet, to be filled out by authors, prior to resubmitting a revision, to enable them to address comments by others before attempting a rewrite. Thus, Appendices B and C offer a check against a hasty revision.

Features of the Second Edition

The aim of this second edition is precisely the same as the first: to offer instructors a fitting companion to introductory-level courses that details how to read, evaluate, and respond in writing to philosophical works. There are a number of other books on the market with similar aims, yet I have found none that balances concern for reading, evaluating, and writing philosophy in a compendious, user-friendly format—hence, the motivation for a second edition to this book. Some books err on the side of succinctness, where the material, lacking explanation, is too dense and requires continual explication of the instructor. Other books err on the side of prolixity, where the material, explained to death, makes a book out of what was meant to be a booklet and, thereby, keeps students away from primary-source materials.

With the intention of avoiding both extremes, I have aimed in this second edition to provide instructors with a succinct, though non-trivial, companion booklet for an introductory course in philosophy. The features of this edition are as follows:

Features Retained

- Modular Format: The material is presented in modules—short, self-teaching units that are designed to make critical evaluation of philosophy student-friendly. The large number of modules and small size of each make for ready and easy assimilation of the material in them.
- Succinctness of Presentation: As this is principally meant to be a companion booklet to introductory-level courses in philosophy, it is important that the book remain a booklet and not strive to be a course in its own right. To that end, succinctness is crucial. In addition, this edition is also not meant to be a workbook, so modules contain no practice exercises at their end. It is expected that instructors will draw from primary-source materials for exercises (e.g., for putting arguments into standard form or for diagramming them; Modules 5-6 and 12-13, respectively).
- Helpful Appendices: Students have told me that they have found the appendices, especially B and C, to be very helpful. Thus, I have retained those appendices.
- I have kept the modules on argument diagramming, both because some instructors find diagramming arguments to be the *sine qua non* of reconstruction and because I believe that those modules offer tools for diagramming that are uncommon in philosophical texts on critical reasoning.

Features Added

- New Structure: The general presentation of the material has been altered to better accommodate its three main aims: reading, evaluating, and writing philosophy. Thus, Parts II through IV are entitled Reading Philosophy, Evaluating Philosophy, and Writing Philosophy.
- Clearer Exposition: Though the first edition, I believe, achieved its aim of clarity of exposition, this new edition aims for improved clarity through the addition of new illustrations and examples as well as a different, more student-friendly formatting of the material.
- New Modules: There are three additional modules in this edition. They are added to amplify on what I perceive to be underdeveloped points made in the first edition.

How to Use This Book

This book is best used as the critical-thinking component to an introductory-level class, such as Introduction to Philosophy, Environmental Philosophy, or Humans and Society. As such, it is recommended that instructors use the book to supplement assigned primary-source readings along the way (assigning, for instance, the first four, easy-to-read modules in the first two weeks of the course and other modules of an instructor's choosing along the way). As the course unfolds, instructors may wish to go over and expand on points made in the more technical modules on argument reconstruction—Modules 6, 12, and 13—by illustrating, say, how to put an argument from Plato's *Philebus* into standard form or how to diagram that argument to show its complexity and its main conclusion. Of course, instructors can use the book just as well without covering the more technical material in Modules 6, 12, and 13. The modules on philosophical essays prove invaluable, when using the book in this manner.

A second way to use the book is as the main text of a course on critical thinking. In this manner, instructors will cover the material of the book seriatim and choose, along with it, a couple of other short primary-source works, like Descartes' *Meditations* or Mill's *On Liberty*, and then teach students just how to read, evaluate, and respond critically to them. Breaking down arguments into standard form and diagramming will be foci of such a course. So, too, will be critical essays to the primacy-source works at term's end.

A third way to use this book is merely to assign it as a supplement to philosophy courses that are writing-intensive. Here the aim will be to have students, during the course of the term, read only those nine modules that concern writing philosophical essays. Many students believe that there are no objective features of a good critical essay. These nine modules debunk that myth. Thus, they free instructors from spending a quarter of their course covering the fundamentals of essay writing—something students were supposed to learn prior to college.

Acknowledgments

I would like to thank my students for their many editorial comments over the years on the first edition. I would also like to thank Jon Sisk and the many fine people at Rowman & Littlefield.

PART I
INTRODUCTORY CONCERNS

MODULE 1
What Is Philosophy?

Traditionally, and I might even say superficially, "philosophy" has been defined as the "love of wisdom," and "philosophers" as "lovers of wisdom." That, at least, is what we find when we look into the etymology of the words. (The Greek word *philein* means "to like" or "to love" and *sophia* means "wisdom.") These definitions, however, do not help much in telling us just what it is that philosophers do. Many people, I suppose, believe that philosophers are rather disagreeable people, who saunter about and try to show others that they have no grounds for anything they happen to hold as true. Others think, as I have often heard, everyone is a philosopher to some degree.

While it is certainly true that philosophers argue much of the time and that all people discuss philosophical issues some of the time, it is not true that philosophers argue ceaselessly to no fruitful end or that everyone is a philosopher. There is a point to philosophical "contentiousness": Philosophical argument attempts to clarify matters by ridding everyday language of ambiguity and vagueness. What is the payoff? It is a better grasp of the issues and perhaps even a solution to some mulish problem.

All of us recognize the vital importance of the various arts and sciences. Art and its various means of expression add fullness, variety, beauty, and even flavor to our lives. Science continually makes discoveries that contribute to our health and our comfort. We take art and science for granted, yet the thought of life without either of them is too gruesome for most of us to entertain.

What makes art so special to us? Why do we trust the discoveries of the sciences? Answers to these questions require that we delve into philosophy. Philosophy takes what seems plainly true or obvious and subjects it to scrutiny for the sake of deeper understanding. For instance, we take it for granted when a study suggests that vitamin E slows aging and guards against cancer. We exercise caution when a study indicates that cell-phone use may be linked to brain cancer. What, after all, do we really know about the science behind vitamin E or cell phones? Because of ignorance or a sense of security that comes through thinking that others have answers that we do not have, often we blindly follow when authorities like scientists speak.

However, the study of philosophy gives us the analytic tools to dissect what scientists do and open it to critical examination. Moreover, what it does to sci-

3

ence, it does to all other disciplines—even itself. Yes, there is even a philosophy of philosophy, called "metaphilosophy." Philosophy takes our most fundamental principles and beliefs and asks us for a justification of them. It invites us to ask questions such as: What, if anything, is the best form of political life for humans? How ought we to live our lives? Does god exist? Behind the veneer of things that continually change, is anything unchanging? What is love? What is beauty? Philosophy, then, is the science of sciences.

METHODS OF PHILOSOPHY

Why do we engage in philosophy? Perhaps no better answer exists than that given by Aristotle in the fourth century B.C.: We are naturally curious animals. Yet to engage in philosophy is not merely a matter of being curious about things. It requires that our curiosity be expressed through questions and answers in a manner that is both systematic and critical. Thus, the methods of philosophy are many. I enumerate some of the most important below.

PHILOSOPHY IS ANALYTIC. It analyzes our most basic assumptions as we attempt to understand ourselves and the world around us.

PHILOSOPHY IS NORMATIVE. It appeals to rules or precepts that distinguish correct from incorrect human thinking and behavior.

PHILOSOPHY IS CRITICAL. It challenges traditional cannons of belief to get at truth or further our understanding of some issue.

PHILOSOPHY IS SYNTHETIC. It aims to synthesize our views of ourselves and our world in a coherent and systematic manner.

PHILOSOPHY IS RATIONAL. It insists that reasons be given for what we believe and that consistency, simplicity, coherence, and order of thoughts are desirable.

PHILOSOPHY IS IMAGINATIVE. It invites us to explore and examine new ways of looking at philosophical problems and issues.

PHILOSOPHY IS RESOURCEFUL. It requires us to consider what is logically possible, but asks only that we act as circumstances allow.

TRADITIONAL BRANCHES OF PHILOSOPHY

Philosophy has historically been divided into five chief sub-disciplines: metaphysics, epistemology, aesthetics, ethics, and logic.

METAPHYSICS is the study of what is real. Metaphysics is an attempt at a coherent account of all that exists; the study of the most general and pervasive characteristics of the universe; or the study of ultimate reality.

EPISTEMOLOGY is the study of knowledge. Epistemology examines the origins, presuppositions, nature, extent, and validity of knowledge.

AESTHETICS is the study of beauty and related concepts. Aesthetics asks questions such as: What is art? Are all beautiful things equally beautiful? Is there such a thing as aesthetic sensibility?

ETHICS is the study of morality or the best manner of living. Ethics examines concepts related to practical reasoning, such as freedom of will, choice, virtue, duty, good, and right.

LOGIC is the study of the principles of reasoning. Logic is a normative discipline that is used as a tool for all sciences, even philosophy.

Most major philosophy departments offer courses in political philosophy, philosophy of mind, philosophy of science, and philosophy of language as well.

Yet today philosophers study a diverse field of practical issues from feminism and race relations to conflict resolution, sex and love, and death. In a sense, philosophers take many of the same questions that arise with respect to the "big five" and apply them to a broad array of today's topics of study.

MODULE 2
Philosophy & Critical Reasoning

APPLIED PHILOSOPHY

Applied philosophy is a non-traditional approach to philosophical inquiry in that its subject matter draws from everyday-life concerns. Contemporary issues in applied philosophy are in the areas of sex and love, politics, gender, race, environmental philosophy, medical ethics, peace and conflict resolution, and sport, to name just some.

Why is there a need for applied philosophy? The reason is simple. We benefit greatly by applying philosophical methods to the issues that confront us in our daily lives. Today there is great debate on issues like drug-use, free-market capitalism, environmental sustainability, the spread of AIDS, globalization, global warming, and gender equality. Unsurprisingly, those issues also invite rigorous debate, even among experts, which makes it unreasonable, even irresponsible, to speak with absolute certainty on them. Let us consider the morality of cloning. Many of us feel an undeniable repugnance for that technology. Our repugnance seems grounded by certain "intuitively correct" feelings that cloning is morally wrong. Yet it is difficult to put into words why that is so. Repugnance, of course, is no justification for moral incorrectness. Nonetheless, we must make decisions on such issues. If not, they are left in the hands of others to decide them for us.

WHAT IS A CRITICAL ATTITUDE?

"A man never tells you anything until you contradict him," wrote George Bernard Shaw. What Shaw meant was that the way people handle being contradicted says much about the sort of persons they are. Uncritical, unreflective persons immediately become indignant, when contradicted. Critical reasoners look at being contradicted as a challenge. Let me elaborate.

Everyone has a unique depiction of the way the world is. For some, that picture is fixed through an uncritical acceptance of a notion of how things are that is perhaps handed down to them through their parents or a form of religious indoctrination. Such unreflective people are always unbendingly convinced that their picture is correct. Yet with the slightest provocation, it becomes clear that they are not in the least concerned with truth; instead they are content just to have a picture, whether it is coherent or incoherent. Unreflective acceptance would be fine, were there not so many religions saying so many different things or if there were some guarantee that parental wisdom is infallible.

Fortunately, such completely unreflective people are rare and most of us, through experience, have learned that things are not always as they seem to be or as we want them to be. We are perplexed by so many different "explanations" given by so many "authorities" of how the world works. We have come to realize that many of the things that we have at one time accepted as true have been shown at some later time to be at odds with reality. Thus, we exercise due caution before accepting some claim as true, for we want good reasons or the right sort of evidence for it. Consequently, for most of us, our picture of the world is a work-in-progress. We are continually taking in new data and restructuring our picture of things in order to accommodate those data in a consistent and coherent way. We have, in short, a critical attitude.

As is the case with any normative discipline, there are rules and guidelines for a correct approach to critical reasoning. This booklet attempts to introduce you to these rules in a manner that is friendly, informative, and perhaps even life-changing. So-ooo...

LET'S GET CRITICAL!

There are a number of reasons—some practical, others not so practical but no less desirable—to adopt a critical attitude and to use critical reasoning. I enumerate some below.

Conflict Resolution

"The greatest of all fortunes," Freud wrote in a letter to friend Wilhelm Fliess, "is either good humor or a clear mind." One way to attain mental clarity is by resolving internal conflicts and critical-reasoning skills are the best tools for resolution of conflict at any level. Critical reasoning is an appeal to reasons and evidence, not persuasion through force, bribery, fear, or emotion. It is, therefore, an essential tool for resolving internal conflict, conflict between yourself and others, and conflict within and between groups of people—e.g., religious factions, political parties, or nations.

Success in Attaining Goals

Critical-reasoning skills can be put to use in bettering personal decisions in an effort to reach your aims in life. Making decisions based on good reasons is always preferable to acting on a whim or acting according to someone else's advice, which may not be in your best interest. Deliberative calculation makes success at attaining goals much more likely than does non-deliberative action. Deliberative calculation also puts you in a better position to determine precisely what goals are the right goals to have in life.

Internal Stability

"Reason ... represents or rather constitutes a single formal interest, the interest in harmony," said George Santayana. A critical attitude helps you to strive for harmony of the sort Santayana spoke of through internal stability—a type of mental solidity characterized, first, by proportioning conviction of belief to evidence and, second, by holding consistency in highest regard. Proportioning conviction of belief to the evidence on its behalf is a commitment to see the world as it is, not to impose your own structure or values on it. Holding consistency in highest regard is a commitment not to accept readily some claim as true, if it conflicts with other claims that you have good grounds for believing to be true.

Open-Mindedness

"It is the mark of an educated mind," Aristotle said, "to be able to entertain a thought without accepting it." A commitment to critical reasoning requires you to consider openly the merit of alternative views that are inconsistent with, and pose a challenge to, your own views. In such a manner, you are challenged to defend your views. Through such challenges, you may find that your views are correct or that they require reconsideration. If they require reconsideration, they might have to be altered or, in extreme cases, discarded.

Fallibility

Open-mindedness, of course, requires fallibility. As a critical reasoner, you assume fallibility—a willingness to entertain all reasonable claims as true, if only provisionally, in an effort to increase one's own understanding as well as that of all parties involved. Thus, a critical attitude is essentially an unselfish attitude. With fallibility, however, comes a sort of mental freedom—a "mental power ... emancipated from the leading strings of others," as Dewey writes—which uncritical and unreflective sorts can never have.

Fullness of Understanding

Exposing your own position to criticism enables you to gain the fullest possible understanding of its strengths and flaws. Knowing the flaws of your position enables you to eliminate or, at least, address them. If critical exposure shows your position to be untenable, then you will be able to escape error through greater understanding of your position, which is, in the words of the poet Homer, a true "gold-for-bronze exchange."

Intellectual Integrity

"All our dignity consists ... in thought," said Blaise Pascal. "Let us endeavour then to think well...." Pascal was referring to a sort of intellectual integrity that comes through thinking well and clearly. Critical reasoning, thus, is a commitment to an honest search for truth, conceptual clarification, or heightened under-standing. Overall, demanding evidence before believing something to be true is not something to be reviled, but something of which you should be proud.

PART II
READING PHILOSOPHY

MODULE 3
General Form of a Philosophical Work

Bertrand Russell said in *The Wisdom of the West*:

> We may note one peculiar feature of philosophy. If someone asks the question what is mathematics, we can give him a dictionary definition, let us say the science of number, for the sake of argument.... Definitions may be given in this way of any field where a body of definite knowledge exists. But philosophy cannot be so defined. Any definition is controversial and already embodies a philosophic attitude. The only way to find out what philosophy is, is to do philosophy.

Russell's quote demonstrates the peculiarity of philosophy. Where a definite body of knowledge exists in a field of inquiry—say, in biology or anthropology—we may circumscribe that discipline with a term, say "biology," and apply to it a definition that has, at least, provisional status. Philosophy, since it does not comprise a definite body of knowledge, is incapable of such a circumscription. Any definition already presupposes a philosophical slant.

Today two main philosophical camps, as it were, exist: analytic philosophy and continental philosophy. I cannot attempt to distinguish fully the differences between these two camps—any attempt will falter—and so I offer merely a rough and admittedly inadequate sketch of a few differences between the two below that focuses on how each approaches philosophical problems.

First, *analytic philosophers* have a *problems-of-philosophy approach* to philosophy—i.e., they tend to investigate philosophical problems independently of the circumstances in which they arose. That suggests that analytic philosophers see philosophical problems as problems that do not plague humans, just because of their humanness. Philosophical problems are real problems for any sort of creature in possession of rationality. Second, with a focus on rationality, the analytic tradition is driven by the notion that words are not hopelessly plastic. Words have definite meanings, though those meanings may sometimes be obscured by *vagueness* (when a word's meaning is unclear) or *ambiguity* (when a word has more than one precise meaning). Thus, analytic philosophers focus on language and logic as well as clarity and succinctness of philosophical expression through argument. Finally, analytic philosophers tend to view the natural sciences as making discoveries about the nature of the world

and, thus, as progressive, while they tend to view philosophy as foundational—
i.e., as the science of sciences.

In contrast, *continental philosophers*—comprising, for instance, existential-
ists, critical theorists, phenomenologists, idealists, hermeneuticists, and deconstructionists—tend to have a *history-of-philosophy approach*—i.e., they see philosophical problems as problems that arise in particular episodes of human history and any investigation of such problems must take into consideration those
uniquely human circumstances. Context is crucial to understanding a philosophical problem. So, too, is text. Hermeneuticists, for instance, see meaning not in
words or actions, but in *how* words or actions are interpreted. Interpretation,
thus, has an inescapable social dimension. Deconstructionists see an "other" in
words and actions that is ostensibly absent, but latently present. For them, meaning is always confused and requires social analysis to reveal the concealed other.
In the main, continental philosophers do not believe that science is in the busi-
ness of making discoveries about the world. Also, they do not believe that philosophy has a special, foundational status among disciplines.

This booklet, written with respect for the continental tradition, is written in
the analytic tradition. Philosophical problems, given that philosophy is, in a
sense, the "science of sciences," are problems of a different sort than, say, problems of science, religion, or even those of everyday living. Philosophical problems differ from problems of science in that scientists use empirical, not a priori,
methods to work toward their solutions. Philosophical problems differ from religious problems in that religionists often appeal to faith, revelation, or authority
in lieu of reason. Philosophical problems differ from everyday-life problems in
that everyday-life issues are particular and near to human concerns, in a manner
of speaking, while philosophical problems are general and seem somehow distant from us. Philosophers ask questions such as "How do we know that we can
know?" and "Is life meaningful or meaningless?" and those sorts of questions,
being of a fundamental sort, come to have a permanent grip, at least, on certain
sorts of persons.

TWO AIMS OF A PHILOSOPHICAL ESSAY OR BOOK

Given some notion of what a philosophical problem is, the remarks in the remainder of this module will focus on how to read philosophy critically. To that
end, elements like philosophical creativity, enjoyment, and vision may get short
shrift.

Elaborating on an Existing Philosophical Problem

In the main, philosophical works are elaborations of existing, entrenched philosophical problems—some of which have been around for millennia.

Consider this example from the introduction of "Thomas Jefferson's View
of Equal Social Opportunity" by Robert Heslep.

It is easily recognized that Thomas Jefferson held to a notion of equal social opportunity. ... [T]here are two widely accepted arguments to the effect that he did not hold to the notion very firmly. Noting that his plan for public education in Virginia provides free elementary schooling for all impecunious students in that state but provides free secondary and university education for only the superior of these students, critics of his educational thought frequently charge that, in constructing the plan, Jefferson did not adhere to an idea of equal educational opportunity and, therefore, was not averse to violating his notion of equal social opportunity. And, pointing out that he definitely regarded Negroes as inferior to Caucasians, critics of his political thought have concluded, at times, that Jefferson never intended for the Negroes in the United States to have the same chances as the Caucasians in the nation and, hence, did not intend that *all* human beings should have equal social opportunity.

Both of these arguments are wrong. The reason why they are is that they involve, in one way or another, a faulty comprehension of Jefferson's view of equal social opportunity. Accordingly, a clarification is in order.

The first sentence of the introduction indicates that the philosophical problem concerns Jefferson's account of equal social opportunity. Heslep, then, mentions two general directions in the scholarly literature that point to inconsistency of word and deed concerning Jefferson's views of social equality. First, there are those scholars who charge Jefferson with providing only superior persons access to higher education. Second, there are those scholars who charge Jefferson with racial discrimination. (He explains why those accounts are misguided in sections three and four of his paper.) Here we note that confusion among scholars is the issue with which Heslep contends. The author asserts that both groups of critics incriminate Jefferson even though they have a faulty grasp of his notion of social equality.

Disclosure of a New Philosophical Problem

Often, however, authors claim to have discovered a new problem, worth some philosophical ink. In such cases, the authors will indicate the problem early in the work—in books, most often in the preface or introduction—and then offer some justification for the problem—i.e., some argument that shows why the problem is a genuine, not a pseudo, philosophical problem.

Let us consider this passage from James Sterba in the first three paragraphs of his introduction in *The Triumph of Practice over Theory in Ethics.*

Ethics appears to be unlike other areas of inquiry. After all, we cannot find contemporary defenders of Ptolemy, Copernicus, or even Isaac Newton, all claiming to have the best theory of the physics of celestial motion. ... But we can find contemporary defenders of Aristotle, Immanuel Kant, and John Stuart Mill, for example, all claiming to have the best theory of ethics. Of course, significant disagreements remain in other areas of inquiry, but the extent of disagreement appears to be much greater in ethics.

One explanation ... is that there is little or nothing that can really be established in ethics. .... According to this account, ethics simply lacks the resources to defeat any of the contending theories, and so they all remain live options. Obviously, this explanation does not put ethics in a favorable light.

Another explanation, the one I defend in this book, is that traditional theories of ethics, be they Aristotelian, Kantian, Millian, or whatever, have come to be revised and reformed in such a way that, at least in their most morally defensible formulations, they no longer differ in the practical requirement they endorse.... In searching for what is morally defensible in these traditional theories, contemporary defenders have jettisoned much of what had distinguished these traditional theories from each other.

First, we find a clear statement of the philosophical problem in the first paragraph of the book: Ethics is not only different from other areas of inquiry, but there is also significant disagreement among adherents of schools of thought. Next, we find a justification of the philosophical nature of the problem implicit in the very statement of the problem (in paragraph one). I flesh it out in argument form to make it plain.

1) Most genuine fields of inquiry do not tolerate significant disagreement.
2) Ethics does.
3) So, ethics is either not an area of genuine inquiry (paragraph 2) or the disagreement is more apparent than real (paragraph 3).[1]

Finally, Sterba gives his solution, plainly marked out by "the one I defend in this book," in the third paragraph. That is confirmed by what he says later on the fifth page of the introduction, "In this book, I argue that the relatively formal tenets shared by Aristotelians, Kantians, and Millians respectively, when correctly understood, do little to divide these groups from one another, at least at the practical level, with regard to the most morally defensible formulations of their views."

Consider, also, the beginning of an essay by Isaiah Berlin, "Two Concepts of Liberty."

To coerce a man is to deprive him of freedom—freedom from what? Almost every moralist in human history has praised freedom. Like happiness and goodness, like nature and reality, the meaning of this term is so porous that there is little interpretation that it seems able to resist. I do not propose to discuss either the history or the more than two hundred senses of this protean word recorded by historians of ideas. I propose to examine no more

---

1. One can clearly see a third approach—ethics is a non-trivially *unique* area of genuine inquiry—which Sterba does not consider.

than two of the senses—but those central ones, with a great deal of human history behind them, and, I dare say, still to come. The first of these political senses of freedom or liberty ..., which ... I shall call the 'negative' sense, is involved in the answer to the question, 'What is the area within which the subject—a person or group of persons—is or should be left to do or be what he is able to do or be, without interference by other persons?' The second, which I shall call the 'positive' sense, is involved in the answer to the question, 'What, or who, is the source of control or interference that can determine someone to do, or be, this rather than that?' The two questions are clearly different, even though the answers to them may overlap.

Note how the philosophical problem is cleanly spelled out early in the passage: Everyone praises the merits of freedom, yet the term is "so porous" that it seems to accommodate any interpretation. Second, we find a justification of the problem in an argument that may be spelled out as follows (the conclusion being implicit):

1) Everyone praises the merits of "freedom."
2) The term is so vague that it accommodates any interpretation.
3) Words so vague are meaningless, or nearly so.
4) So, the praise on behalf of "freedom" is meaningless.

Finally, note that Berlin's proposed solution is modest. He wishes merely to examine both a "positive" and "negative" sense of "freedom" in an attempt to make the word and essays involving it a bit less porous.

MODULE 4
Four Helpful Steps

Reading philosophy is, in some measure, like getting physically fit. Getting physically fit is not easy. It is not a matter of joining a gym and working out each day. To get fit, one has to know what one is doing and be efficient at it. Efficiency at fitness also requires time away from the gym to rest and recover. Likewise, reading philosophical works is not easy. Here, also, knowledge and efficiency are critical. So, too, is rest and, as it were, recovery. Some philosophical notions take time, plenty of time, to digest.

Not only are philosophical topics distant from everyday-life concerns, but philosophical works are often dense, technical, and obscure. It is not uncommon to hear students grumble that they have had to read a work "more than once" before they could figure out what the author was trying to say. I console them by telling them that that is standard practice for most professors of philosophy, myself included.

This module offers four steps to enable you to become more efficient at reading philosophy.

STEP 1
EXAMINE THE TITLE OF THE ARTICLE OR BOOK.

This step is so obvious that most students fail to consider it. The title of a philosophical essay or book should give you a reliable indication of what the essay or book is about. Caution is in order here. Some authors try to be cutesy with their title and the result is that the title is uninformative or misleading to the intended audience. Other authors give their book or essay two titles and it is only the secondary title that is informative. Good publishing companies often force authors not to be cutesy, if being cutesy means being uninformative or misleading. Unfortunately, these days, in the case of books, being cutesy, even outrageous, is increasingly popular, because it sells books. What is the moral? Consider the title in most instances as a reliable, not infallible, guide to the topic of the philosophical work.

Let us take, as illustrations, the titles of the two essays—"Thomas Jefferson's View of Equal Social Opportunity" and "Two Concepts of Liberty"—and of the book—*The Triumph of Theory over Practice in Ethics*—in the prior module. All titles are concise and informative. There is nothing cutesy, nothing misleading.

STEP 2
IDENTIFY THE AUTHOR'S THESIS.

What is a thesis? "Thesis" comes from the Greek noun, transliterated the same way, and literally means a "setting," "placing," "putting forth", or "proposition." When an author of a philosophical work puts forth a thesis, that author is literally putting forth something—i.e., a proposition in sentence form that needs to be defended by arguments.

In essays, the thesis should come relatively early in the essay. In books, the thesis is usually stated in the preface or introduction, where the author sets up his motivation for writing the book. Examine closely the title and table of contents also. The thesis statement should always be written in such a way to make it clear to readers that it is the thesis statement. This, however, is not always the case, so be cautious. Often what an author intends to do is written out in several sentences.

Let us examine again Berlin's opening paragraph from his essay on freedom.

> To coerce a man is to deprive him of freedom—freedom from what? Almost every moralist in human history has praised freedom. Like happiness and goodness, like nature and reality, the meaning of this term is so porous that there is little interpretation that it seems able to resist. I do not propose to discuss either the history or the more than two hundred senses of this protean word recorded by historians of ideas. *I propose to examine no more than two of the senses—but those central ones, with a great deal of human history behind them, and, I dare say, still to come. The first of these political senses of freedom or liberty ..., which ... I shall call the 'negative' sense, is involved in the answer to the question, 'What is the area within which the subject—a person or group of persons—is or should be left to do or be what he is able to do or be, without interference by other persons?' The second, which I shall call the 'positive' sense, is involved in the answer to the question, 'What, or who, is the source of control or interference that can determine someone to do, or be, this rather than that?'* The two questions are clearly different, even though the answers to them may overlap.

Here Berlin, after stating the philosophical problem, tells his readers first what he does not intend to do—to discuss the history or the numerous senses of "freedom"—and then what he does intend to do—state and elaborate on two senses of "freedom" in an effort to clear up philosophical confusion in political philosophy. Note here that the thesis, italicized above, is spelled out in several sentences.

Consider also Kathryn Pyne Addelson's, "Equality and Competition: Can Sports Make a Woman of a Girl?"

> Issues of social justice are among the most intellectually challenging to both the ethicist and philosopher of law, especially when there appear to be permanent, biologically determined differences of ability and potential among

the people and between the groups for whom justice is sought. Such is the case between men and women in the realm of sports. The problem of providing justice in this area has been the topic of popular magazine articles, federal and state legislation, adjudication and philosophical contemplation. But the heart of the matter has yet to be discussed. I will attempt to do this [i.e., get at the heart of the matter] by first reviewing some of the current issues in this area, then exploring the relationship between the use and exchange values of athletic participation, and finally proposing a radical solution which is defended on utilitarian, egalitarian and Rawlsian ethical grounds. The result will be an approach to promoting social justice and equality amongst biologically diverse groups which may be applicable beyond the area of sports.

The first four sentences state the philosophical problem: gender equality in sports. The fourth indicates that all attempts to solve this problem have missed the crux of the matter. The last two sentences state what the author intends to do in a clear and systematic manner, though no precise articulation of a thesis is given—i.e., the radical solution is not stated.

STEP 3
LOOK FOR ARGUMENTS IN SUPPORT OF THE THESIS.

In essays, look at the overall structure of a paper for support of the thesis. Good writers will use their thesis and introductory paragraph(s) as a guide to the format of the remainder of their paper. For instance, if the thesis is compound, each of the sections of the paper may represent one of the components of the thesis. Arguments on behalf of the thesis, however, can be contained in one or many sections of the paper.

In books, look at the table of contents for guidance. It is in a straightforward sense an author's outline of the book's content. Different chapters can contain different arguments for a thesis or all arguments can come in one chapter or a few.

One suggestion is this. Beginning with the thesis, make a general outline of the paper or book. For a book, be content with a broad outline. Next, fill in your outline by fleshing out each of the main arguments with a second or third reading (or more, if necessary).

STEP 4
EVALUATE OF ARGUMENTS ON BEHALF OF THESIS.

The final step for reading philosophy concerns critical analysis of the arguments given on its behalf. That requires much more discussion than I can give in this module and will be the focus of later modules. For now, be content with being sure that you have faithfully captured an author's main line of argument.

Given the denseness and complexity of most philosophical works, do not be frustrated if you fail to grasp what an author is getting at in a single reading or even in a few readings. Settle for a comfortable feel for what is being argued, and then reread the work in an effort to flesh out precisely the line of argument. Do not be frustrated by the time and effort this takes, for your aim is a full grasp of the content, and that, you may come to find, is its own reward.

Overall, critical analysis of philosophical material, like any other skill, takes practice to develop and practice takes time. Most importantly, expect to make numerous mistakes along the way. Ask your instructor for help, if necessary.

PART III
EVALUATING PHILOSOPHY

SECTION A
Argument Recognition & Reconstruction

MODULE 5
Elements of Argument Recognition

SENTENCES V. STATEMENTS

What Is a Sentence?

A *SENTENCE* IS A SYNTACTIC CONJUNCTION OF WORDS IN A PARTICULAR LANGUAGE THAT IS GRAMMATICALLY SOUND ACCORDING TO THE RULES OF THAT LANGUAGE.

Examples of proper sentences:

1) Roxanne tends to collect brummagems.
2) Is the wizard really a good wizard?
3) Get yourself ready for Scrabble!
4) Try the Teriyaki Chicken.

Of these, each is a grammatically sound string of words in English and each communicates something that is readily accessible to another English-speaking person. The first is a *declarative sentence* in that it admits of truth or falsity. The second is a *question*. The third is an *order*. The last is a *suggestion*.

Examples of improper sentences:

1) Roxanne tends brummagems to often collect to.
2) Wizard really good?
3) Yourself for ready get Scrabble!
4) The Teriyaki try Chicken.

The first ends in a preposition ("to") that has no object and splits its infinite ("to often collect" should read "to collect often"). The second example lacks a verb. The third and fourth have all the components for a sentence, but the ordering violates proper English syntax.

What Is a Statement?

A *STATEMENT* IS THE MEANING OF A DECLARATIVE SENTENCE.

Like all declarative sentences, every statement admits of truth or falsity in that it asserts, rightly or wrongly, something is the case.

27

Examples of statements:

1) The 5:15 train is running on time.
2) The tenor's voice was flat last night.
3) The 5:15 train is not running on time.
4) If the tenor's voice was flat last night, the show was a failure.
5) The 5:15 train is running on time or it is not.
6) The tenor's voice was flat last night and the 5:15 train is running on time.

As a statement is really the propositional content or meaning of a declarative sentence, I shall use the words "statement" and "proposition" as synonymous throughout.

Let us now distinguish simple from compound statements.

A *SIMPLE STATEMENT* IS A STATEMENT THAT DOES NOT HAVE ANOTHER STATEMENT AS A PART.

For instance, the first three illustrations are simple statements.

Given the definition of "simple statement," a compound statement may be defined as follows:

A *COMPOUND STATEMENT* IS A STATEMENT THAT HAS AT LEAST ONE SIMPLE STATEMENT AS A PART.

Compound statements comprise negations, conditionals, disjunctions, and conjunctions (examples three through six, above).

First, there are negations.

A *NEGATIVE STATEMENT* IS A SIMPLE STATEMENT THAT IS NEGATED.

There are many ways to negate a simple sentence. The statement "The 5:15 train is not running on time" can be expressed also thus:

1) It is not the case that the 5:15 train is running on time.
2) It is false that the 5:15 train is running on time.
3) There is no way that the 5:15 train is running on time.
4) The 5:15 fails to be running on time.

Next, there are conditionals or if-then statements.

A *CONDITIONAL STATEMENT* IS A STATEMENT, WHOSE PARTS, CALLED "ANTECEDENT" AND "CONSEQUENT," ARE LINKED BY THE WORDS "IF" AND "THEN," RESPECTIVELY, OR OTHER WORDS WITH EQUIVALENT CONDITIONAL FORCE.

A conditional, because antecedent and consequent are conditionally related, is not meaningful if the truth values of the antecedent and the consequent are analyzed separately. For instance, the statement "If there is no deity, then there is no point of existence" is neither asserting the antecedent, "There is no deity," as true, nor is it asserting the consequent, "There is no point of existence," as true. Instead, it is asserting that if the antecedent is true, so too is the consequent— i.e., a *relationship* between the two parts. So, do not break conditionals into separate statements.

Next, there are disjunctions.

A *DISJUNCTIVE STATEMENT* IS A STATEMENT, WHOSE PARTS, CALLED "DISJUNCTS," ARE LINKED BY THE WORD "OR."

Like conditionals, the parts of disjunctions cannot meaningfully be analyzed independently of the statement as a whole. For instance, the statement "It is best to lie, to dissemble, or feign insanity" is true when one of its disjuncts is true, for the disjuncts here are exclusive. In contrast, the statement "The maple is either tall or full" is true when one disjunct is true or both are true, for here the disjuncts are not exclusive. Thus, a disjunction is true, if at least one of its disjunctive parts is true. So, do not break disjunctions into separate statements.

Finally, there are conjunctions.

A *CONJUNCTIVE STATEMENT* IS A STATEMENT, WHOSE PARTS, CALLED "CONJUNCTS," ARE LINKED BY "AND" OR SOME OTHER WORD WITH (ROUGHLY) EQUIVALENT CONNECTIVE FORCE.

For instance, the statement "You ought to tell the truth, not to lie, and to be consistent in your words and actions" is asserting three things—each of its conjuncts—and, thus, is not true unless each of its conjuncts is true. In other words, the truth value of the statement as a whole is false whenever any one of its parts is false. Since it is asserting three separate statements, it should be broken into three separate claims.

Module 13 contains a fuller analysis of the three types.

Statement/Sentence Distinction

How do statements differ from sentences? I offer four guidelines.

DIFFERENT SENTENCES CAN HAVE THE SAME MEANING.

Examples:

1) I love a good, dry stout.
2) A good, dry stout is loved by me.

Here there are two dissimilar declarative sentences that assert exactly the same thing and thus mean the same thing. Having the same meaning translates into being the same statement.

THE SAME SENTENCE CAN HAVE DIFFERENT MEANING.

I am the most penny-pinching person alive.

Consider how the meaning of this changes when it is uttered by different people. Consider also the same sentence with "I," "most," or "penny-pinching" emphasized.

A SENTENCE CAN CONTAIN MORE THAN ONE (SIMPLE) STATEMENT.

Example:

The Countess Ella lost her diamond earrings, but she found them several days later and put them in her safe.

This sentence is really a conjunction of three statements, separated by a comma and the words "but" and "and," that makes three separate claims: "The countess lost her diamond earrings," "She found them several days later," and "She put them in her safe."

ALL STATEMENTS ARE EITHER TRUE OR FALSE, WHILE THAT IS NOT THE CASE FOR ALL SENTENCES (ONLY DECLARATIVE SENTENCES).

Examples:

1) Command: Catch the bus!
2) Proposal: Let's go to the ballpark today.
3) Question: Who is the best fashion designer in Europe?
4) Exclamation: Radical, dude!
5) Suggestion: I suggest you take the train.
6) Declarative Sentence: Natty Zoltan saw his therapist the other day.

Of those, only six is making a statement and, thus, is a proposition—i.e., only the last admits of truth or falsity.

A caveat is in order. Certain questions, *rhetorical questions*, have a function in language that is not interrogatory, but declarative. Thus, rhetorical questions are really not questions at all, but assertions. Consider the following question to a boy, whose finger is on his sister's birthday cake, "Is your finger on the cake?" It is clear that the question is not a request for an answer, but instead an assertion, "I see that your finger is on the carrot cake," or possibly a command, "Get your finger off the carrot cake!" Context will help determine whether or not it is a proposition that forms part of an argument.

WHAT IS AN ARGUMENT?

Arguments and Their Parts

Arguments are commonly understood as verbal disputes between parties, often heated, where each is trying to convince the other of the truth of some point. In such exchanges, the methods of persuasion are virtually limitless. One party may choose reasons, force, pity, or even trickery to get through a point.

For purposes of critical reasoning, that is both too narrow and too broad. It is too narrow, as we shall see, because persuasion is merely one of the aims of critical reasoning. It is too broad, because, when persuasion is the aim, the means of persuasion must be based exclusively on evidence or reasons.

Let us begin with some preliminary definitions:

AN *ARGUMENT* IS A COLLECTION OF PROPOSITIONS WHEREBY EVIDENCE IN THE FORM OF AT LEAST ONE PROPOSITION (THE PREMISE) IS GIVEN IN SUPPORT OF ANOTHER PROPOSITION (THE CONCLUSION).

A *PREMISE* IS A PROPOSITION THAT IS GIVEN AS EVIDENCE FOR ANOTHER PROPOSITION IN AN ARGUMENT.

THE *CONCLUSION* IS A PROPOSITION THAT PURPORTEDLY FOLLOWS FROM THE EVIDENCE IN AN ARGUMENT.

Example:

(1) There must be some gas left in the tank. (2) I filled the tank last night.

Here proposition one, the conclusion, purportedly follows from proposition two, the premise, which is given as evidence for proposition one. Overall, the relationship between premise(s) and the conclusion can be depicted as follows:

Premise(s)
(**P** justifies **C**)

$\downarrow$

Conclusion
(**C** is justified by **P**)

Often, several premises are given on behalf of a single conclusion. Those premises can function independently (where two or more premises work apart from each other and form separate arguments on behalf of the conclusion) or dependently (where two or more premises work together to attempt to justify the conclusion), or there can be some combination of both at play. In short, premises are put forth in order to justify a conclusion—i.e., to show that it is true—while the conclusion in the right sort of argument is justified by the premises.

As later modules will show, large arguments often comprise many smaller arguments within a large, complex argument.

Why We Argue

WE GIVE ARGUMENTS IN AN ATTEMPT TO PERSUADE OTHERS OF THE TRUTH OF SOME STATEMENT THROUGH AN APPEAL TO EVIDENCE OR REASONS IN SUPPORT OF THAT STATEMENT.

Examples:

(1) Norbert committed the crime, (2) since he is a sleazy rogue.

(1) Norbert committed the crime, since (2) he is the owner of the murder weapon and (3) he was at the scene of the crime when the murder occurred.

The second example purports to provide the sort of evidence for the conclusion, "Norbert committed the crime," that is rationally compelling, while example one tries to persuade by what is perhaps an unjustifiable slander against Norbert. That is not to say that the first example is not an argument. It is an argument, but a very bad one.

ARGUMENTS CAN EXTEND OUR KNOWLEDGE OF MATTERS IN WAYS THAT ARE NOT INITIALLY OBVIOUS.

Here persuasion may not be relevant at all. One may be drawing out the consequences of some statement in a manner that discloses new information that was there implicitly all the while.

Examples:

In an infinite universe, every point can be regarded as the center, because every point has an infinite number of stars on each side of it. (Stephen Hawking, *A Brief History of Time*)

Rhonda weighs more than Cindy and Cindy weighs more than Felix, so Rhonda weighs more than Felix.

In both examples, the conclusions (underlined) may not at all be obvious without the evidence of the premises.

Conditions of Acceptance

We can sum upeverything we have said about arguments below:

THE *FUNCTION OF AN ARGUMENT* IS TO ESTABLISH THE TRUTH OF ITS CONCLUSION BY MEANS OF ASSERTING AS TRUE AT LEAST ONE OTHER PROPOSITION (THE PREMISE).

Remember, however, that asserting something to be true is no guarantee that what is being asserted as true is true.

Overall, two *Conditions of Acceptance* must be met before one is in a position to accept a conclusion as true.

CA$_1$: ALL OF THE PREMISES OF AN ARGUMENT MUST BE TRUE (I.E., WHAT IS ASSERTED AS TRUE IN THE PREMISES ACTUALLY IS TRUE).

CA$_2$: THE PREMISES, ASSUMED TRUE, MUST PROVIDE ABSOLUTE SUPPORT (GENERALLY CALLED "DEDUCTIVE VALIDITY") OR AN APPROPRIATE DEGREE OF SUPPORT (GENERALLY CALLED "INDUCTIVE STRENGTH") FOR THE CONCLUSION.

When either of these two principles has not been met, there is good reason *not* to accept the conclusion as true (though it still may be true). When the second condition is violated, we have a fallacy.

A *FALLACY* IS AN ARGUMENT IN WHICH THE PREMISES PURPORT TO BUT DO NOT PROVIDE ADEQUATE SUPPORT FOR THE CONCLUSION.

A more detailed analysis of the function of arguments and fallacies comes later. For now, the aim has been simply to give you a general feel for what an argument is and to define some of the most fundamental terms that we shall be using throughout.

MODULE 6
Standard Argument Form

This module lists 10 steps that help you recognize and reconstruct arguments. Recognition is vital, because argument analysis cannot proceed without it. Reconstruction is vital, because critical analysis of an argument cannot take place without a precise grasp of the structure of the argument.

STEP 1
LOOK FOR AND CIRCLE ALL REASONING INDICATORS IN A PASSAGE YOU SUSPECT CONTAINS AN ARGUMENT.

Reasoning indicators are words that function to designate that a statement is a premise or conclusion of an argument. Here is a fairly complete list of premise and conclusion indicators.

Premise indicators: because, since, for, for the reason that, given that, on account of, assuming that, follows from, supposing, may be inferred from, may be deduced from, as derived from, owing to, seeing that, as, inasmuch as, as shown by, in view of the fact that, as indicated by
Conclusion indicators: therefore, thus, it follows that, may be inferred from, hence, so, implies, entails that, suggests that, demonstrates that, shows, accordingly, is a reason for, this is why, consequently, as a result, proves that, which shows that, for that reason

If a word is a reasoning indicator, it will function exclusively as a premise or a conclusion indicator; no one word has both functions in the English language. However, some words that function as reasoning indicators have other meanings. "Thus," when it is used as a reasoning indicator, always means "therefore." But "thus" can also function adverbially—meaning "in this manner"—and that does not designate a conclusion. "Since" can be a premise indicator or it can merely indicate the passing of time. So, reasoning indicators should not be used as infallible guides for premises or conclusions.
Examples:

Annette likes to think,(thus)she will probably become a philosopher.

Ajax ran the race with intrepidity,(thus)he wore out the soles of his shoes.

(Since)Annette likes to think, she will become a philosopher.

(Since) Roxanne left, Alexander has been sad.

"Thus" functions as a conclusion indicator in example one. There is nothing being argued for in the second. "Since" in the third example picks out a premise. In the last, it merely marks the passing of time.

STEP 2
NUMBER ALL THE STATEMENTS IN THE PASSAGE YOU SUSPECT CONTAINS AN ARGUMENT.

Example:

> The habit of viewing life as a whole is an essential part both of wisdom and of true morality, and is one of the things which ought to be encouraged in education. Consistent purpose is not enough to make life happy, but it is an almost indispensable condition of a happy life. And consistent purpose embodies itself mainly in work. (Bertrand Russell, *Conquest of Happiness*)

With numbers:

> (1) The habit of viewing life as a whole is an essential part both of wisdom and of true morality, *and* (2) is one of the things which ought to be encouraged in education. (3) Consistent purpose is not enough to make life happy, *but* (4) it is an almost indispensable condition of a happy life. *And* (5) consistent purpose embodies itself mainly in work.

The first two sentences contain two statements that are linked by a conjunctive word ("and," "but," "yet," etc.). A conjunctive word is one whose function is just to link together different statements.

STEP 3
UNDERLINE ANY STATEMENT REQUIRING SUPPORT.

Statements requiring support are potential conclusions.
Example:

> Utopian social engineering is fundamentally in conflict with the complexity of the human condition, and social creativity blossoms best when political power is restrained. That basic lesson makes it all the more likely that democracy—and not communism—will dominate the twenty-first century. (Zbigniew Brzezinski, *The Grand Failure*)

Here statements one and two work together as evidence for the third proposition, which really begins after the phrase "that basic lesson makes it all the more likely that," which itself functions as a lengthy conclusion indicator.

With conclusion underlined:

(1) Utopian social engineering is fundamentally in conflict with the complexity of the human condition, and (2) social creativity blossoms best when political power is restrained. (3) That basic lesson makes it all the more likely that <u>democracy—and not communism—will dominate the twenty-first century.</u>

STEP 4
FINDING A POTENTIAL CONCLUSION, LOOK FOR AT LEAST ONE OTHER STATEMENT AIMING TO SUPPORT IT.

Examples:

There was a huge sex scandal at the college. The chancellor will be fired shortly. The women's basketball team lost its 12th-straight game.

There was a huge sex scandal at the college. The chancellor is suspected to be the main person involved in it. The chancellor will be fired shortly.

There are three statements in each example, some of which are statements that could function as the conclusion of an argument. However, only in the second example is there a statement, "The chancellor will be fired shortly," that is given support (the first two propositions). In example one, there is nothing to link any of the three statements together in the form of an argument. We likely have three distinct, unrelated statements. Analysis of example two:

(1) There was a huge sex scandal at the college. (2) The chancellor is suspected to be the main person involved in it. (3) <u>The chancellor will be fired shortly.</u>

What if you know that two statements make up an argument but have difficulty in distinguishing premise from conclusion? Examples:

There is nothing circular about classifying events in terms of their effects; the criterion is both empirical and objective. (B.F. Skinner, *Science and Human Behavior*)

Men are never convinced of your reasons, of your sincerity, of the seriousness of your sufferings, except by your death. So long as you are alive, your case is doubtful; you have a right only to your skepticism. (Albert Camus, *The Fall*)

In both examples, you may know that there is an argument, but not know which proposition is the premise and which is the conclusion. In such cases, use the *Principle of Alternation* as a guide.

IF YOU CANNOT DECIDE WHICH OF TWO STATEMENTS IS THE CONCLUSION, TRY THE FIRST AS THE PREMISE AND THE SECOND AS THE CONCLUSION AND SEE WHETHER THIS MAKES SENSE; IF THIS DOES NOT MAKE SENSE, TRY THE SECOND AS THE PREMISE AND THE FIRST AS THE CONCLUSION.

Analyses:

(1) There is nothing circular about classifying events in terms of their effects; (2) the criterion is both empirical and objective.

(1) Men are never convinced of your reasons, of your sincerity, of the seriousness of your sufferings, except by your death. (2) So long as you are alive, your case is doubtful; you have a right only to your skepticism.

In the first example, the *Principle of Alternation* makes it clear that statement two is a premise for statement one. In the second, statement one is the premise for statement two.

STEP 5
FINDING A POTENTIAL CONCLUSION AND WHAT APPEAR TO BE REASONS FOR IT, ASK IF THE STATEMENT IS FACTUAL OR JUSTIFICATORY.

If it is best taken as factual, then it is likely that there is no argument. If not, then it is likely that there is an argument.

Examples:

(1) The house burned down, (because (2) Olga was smoking in bed.
(1) The house will burn down, (because (2) Olga constantly smokes in bed.

In example one, it would be improper to take "because" as a premise indicator, since the truth of the statement, "The house burned down," is not in question. This statement is factual and needs no *justification*, but it does ask to be *explained*. In other words, its truth is not in question, but its cause is. It is not an argument, but an *explanation*. In this second example, "because" functions to introduce a premise for the statement, "The house will burn down." The future-directedness of this statement gives no doubt about it being in need of justification. Be careful with the word "because." It can designate an argument (the "because" of justification) or an explanation (the "because" of causation).

Overall, when something appears to be an argument, ask yourself whether the would-be conclusion is in question or not. Follow the *Principle of Discernment*.

IF THE WOULD-BE CONCLUSION OF SOMETHING THAT APPEARS TO BE AN ARGUMENT IS PLAINLY FACTUAL, IT IS NOT AN ARGUMENT.

STEP 6
PUT ALL STATEMENTS INTO THEIR SIMPLEST, CLEAREST FORM.

Example:

> If a sleeping person could note that it is raining or judge that his wife is jealous, then why could he not judge that he is asleep? The absurdity of the latter proves the absurdity of the former. (Norman Malcolm, *Dreaming*)

This is hard to reconstruct. The first sentence is rhetorical. It should be rewritten thus: "If a sleeping person could note that it is raining or judge that his wife is jealous, then he would be able to judge that he is asleep." In addition, we find the latter sentence to be really making two statements that have reference to each of the two parts of first sentence, which is a conditional (an if-then statement; see Module 12). The reworked argument looks something like this:

> (1) If a sleeping person could note that it is raining or judge that his wife is jealous, then he would be able to judge that he is asleep. Yet (2) he cannot judge that he is asleep, (so)(3) he cannot judge that it is raining or that his wife is jealous.

STEP 7
CHECK IF THERE ARE UNSTATED PARTS OF THE ARGUMENT AND FILL IN THEM.

Example:

> Noble and beautiful works of art should not be subjected to haste; and this majestic new world is indeed a most noble and beautiful work. (Mark Twain, *The Diary of Adam and Eve*)

What is implicitly concluded here is the statement, "This majestic new world should not be subjected to haste." It is thought to be so obvious that it need not to be explicitly stated. Fleshed out, with brackets to indicate what is implicit, we have:

> (1) Noble and beautiful works of art should not be subjected to haste; and
> (2) this majestic new world is indeed a most noble and beautiful work. [So,
> (3) this majestic new world should not be subjected to haste.]

STEP 8
ELIMINATE IRRELEVANT STATEMENTS.

Examples:

> As there is nothing fundamentally new to be offered in this field since the researches of Freud, Adler, and Stekel, we must content ourselves with corroborating their experiences by citing parallel cases. I have under observation a few cases of this kind which may be worth reporting for their general interest. (C.G. Jung, "On the Significance of Number Dreams")

> There is no respect for the views of others as truth or partial truth; they are from the beginning treated as diseases, sources of vulnerability to disturbance; and the aim [of Skepticism] from the beginning is to subvert them, knock them out. This is so not because, as in Epicureanism, the teacher claims to have the truth already—but because truth is not sought, from any source. (Martha Nussbaum, *The Therapy of Desire*)

In the first example, statement two is the conclusion and the first statement is evidence for it. The third statement does nothing to establish the conclusion's truth. It merely indicates to readers the Jung is about to offer three instances of number dreams that corroborate the work of Freud, Adler, and Stekel. So, we may strike out the final statement.

> (As)(1) there is nothing fundamentally new to be offered in this field since the researches of Freud, Adler, and Stekel, (2) <u>we must content ourselves with corroborating their experiences by citing parallel cases.</u> (3) ~~I have under observation a few cases of this kind which may be worth reporting for their general interest.~~

In the second example, statement four is asserted as something that is not a reason for the conclusion. Only the fifth statement is given as evidence. Yet statement five could equally be seen as evidence for each of the first three statements. Are the first three statements put forth as three conclusions with statement five as support? It is conceivable that they are. Yet Nussbaum's use of "This is so" suggests that only the third statement is the conclusion—otherwise she would probably have begun the second sentence as "These are so...."

> (1) There is no respect for the views of others as truth or partial truth; (2) they are from the beginning treated as diseases, sources of vulnerability to disturbance; and (3) <u>the aim [of Skepticism] from the beginning is to subvert them, knock them out.</u> (This is so) not (because,) (4) ~~as in Epicureanism, the teacher claims to have the truth already~~—but (because) (5) truth is not sought, from any source.

STEP 9
WRITE OUT THE ENTIRE ARGUMENT IN *STANDARD ARGUMENT FORM*.

GUIDELINES FOR STANDARD FORM:

1) Number all statements and order them as follows: Place premises first, then place the conclusion last (prefacing it by the word "so").
2) Use brackets [ ] for implicit statements.
3) Leave out any irrelevant statements.
4) After each conclusion, place numbers in parentheses to indicate how it was derived.

Examples:

(1) Noble and beautiful works of art should not be subjected to haste; and (2) this majestic new world is indeed a most noble and beautiful work. (So) (3) [this majestic new world should not be subjected to haste.]

(1) If it is the nature of the earth as a whole to float on water, the same should be true of every piece of it; but (2) this is plainly contrary to fact, (for) (3) a piece taken at random sinks to the bottom, and (4) the larger it is the quicker it sinks. (Aristotle, *On the Heavens*)

(1) If you quarrel with all your sense-perceptions you will have nothing to refer to in judging even those sense-perceptions which you claim are false. (Epicurus, *Principle Doctrines*)

Example one in standard argument form:

1) Noble and beautiful works of art should not be subjected to haste.
2) This majestic new world is indeed a most noble and beautiful work.
3) [So, this majestic new world should not be subjected to haste.] (1 & 2)

Here the conclusion, bracketed, is not explicit, but implicit.
Example two in standard argument form:

1) If it is the nature of the earth as a whole to float on water, the same should be true of every piece of it.
3) Any random piece sinks to the bottom of water.
2) So, it is not the nature of earth to float on water (1 & 3).

Statement one is a conditional (an "if-then" statement) that should not be broken into separate statements. Also, statement two is not the denial of the whole of statement one, but it denies only the antecedent or "if" part of it. Statement four adds interesting information about the *rate* of fall for earth in water, but that is not relevant for establishing the truth of the conclusion.

Example three in standard argument form:

1) If you quarrel with all your sense-perceptions you will have nothing to refer to in judging even those sense-perceptions which you claim are false.
2) [There must be some standard of judgment for sense-perceptions.]
3) [So, no one can quarrel with all sense-impressions.] (1 & 2)

This example is no argument, since it is only one statement—a lengthy conditional statement—and for there to be an argument there must be at least two statements. Yet it seems clear that it should be taken as an argument, as the antecedent of the condition seems implicitly assumed to be true.

STEP 10
WHEN DONE WITH THE PRIOR STEPS, READ THROUGH THE ARGUMENT TO CHECK YOUR RECONSTRUCTION.

SECTION B
Argument Evaluation

MODULE 7
Setting the Logical Boundaries

Before beginning to evaluate an argument, one must know precisely the meaning of the various statements that are its parts. The slightest "garnishment"—adding, for instance, the word "perhaps" to a statement—can change radically the meaning of a statement in an argument and have a significant impact on one's evaluation of that argument. To that end, this module takes a closer look at statements.

THREE KINDS OF STATEMENTS

Necessary Truth

A *NECESSARY TRUTH* IS A STATEMENT THAT IS TRUE REGARDLESS OF THE WAY THE WORLD IS AT ANY GIVEN TIME.

Example:

> Fabrice either went for a hike in the forest last Wednesday or she failed to do so on that day.

This statement neither asserts that Fabrice took a hike last Wednesday, nor that she did not. It only asserts one *or* the other of two exclusive and exhaustive (i.e., contradictory) states of affairs, so it must be true. Also, as it asserts that one of two contradictory statements is true, without saying which is true, it is wholly uninformative. Thus, a necessary truth lacks empirical content, as its truth does not depend upon the way the world is at any point in time. This statement would be true in any possible world (i.e., a world in which gravity is an inverse-cubed repulsive force or a world where life is possible in conditions of heat in excess of 1000 degrees C). A necessary truth is also called a *tautology*.

Necessary Falsehood

A *NECESSARY FALSEHOOD* IS STATEMENT THAT IS FALSE REGARDLESS OF THE WAY THE WORLD IS AT ANY GIVEN TIME.

Example:

> Marco climbed up the tree at 3 p.m. last Sunday and he did not climb the tree at 3 p.m. last Sunday.

This statement, in contrast to a necessary truth, is very informative—too informative—because it asserts both that a certain state of affairs *and* its contradictory are true, which is impossible. Like a necessary truth, a necessary falsehood lacks empirical content. There is no conceivable world in which this statement would be true. A necessary falsehood is also called a *self-contradiction.*

Contingent Statement

A *CONTINGENT STATEMENT* IS A STATEMENT WHOSE TRUTH IS DETERMINED BY THE STATE OF THE WORLD AT A GIVEN TIME.

Example:

Alexander gave Roxanne the turquoise blender that she had requested.

Of the three types of statements, only contingent statements have empirical content—i.e., their truth depends entirely on the way the world is at a particular time. Here, to see whether this statement is true, we merely try to find out if Alexander gave Roxanne the turquoise blender she had requested.

COMPARING STATEMENTS

Contradictory Statements

TWO STATEMENTS, α AND β, ARE *CONTRADICTORY,* IF WHENEVER α IS TRUE, β IS FALSE, AND WHENEVER α IS FALSE, β IS TRUE.

Examples:

Creation science is the true view of the origin of humans.
Creation science is not the true view of the origin of humans.

These two propositions are contradictory because the second is simply the denial of the first. Thus, the truth-value of the first will always be opposite the other.

Inconsistent Statements

TWO STATEMENTS, α AND β, ARE *INCONSISTENT,* IF BOTH α AND β CANNOT BE TRUE AT THE SAME TIME.

Example:

God created the first organisms on land.
The first organisms arose naturally out of the sea through a slow course of development.

These two propositions are inconsistent in that they both cannot be true at the same time. Note, however, that both statements can be false.

Consistent Statements

TWO STATEMENTS, α AND β, ARE *CONSISTENT,* IF BOTH α AND β CAN BE TRUE AT THE SAME TIME.

Example:

> The first organisms arose from the sea through a slow course of development.
> God is the ultimate cause of all things.

These statements seem inconsistent, but they are not, because it is possible for both statements to be true. A creator could have set up things such that the first organisms arose from the sea.

Equivalent Statements

TWO STATEMENTS, α AND β, ARE *EQUIVALENT,* IF BOTH α AND β DESCRIBE THE EXACT STATE OF AFFAIRS—I.E., WHENEVER α IS TRUE, SO TOO IS β, AND WHENEVER β IS TRUE, SO TOO IS α.

Example:

> Zoltan is a professional athlete.
> Zoltan makes his living playing sports.

Any conceivable world where statement one is true would be a world where statement two is true also. Conversely, any conceivable world where statement one is false would be a world where statement two is false. The truth-value of each is always the same under all possible conditions, because the two sentences mean precisely the same thing.

STATEMENT MODALITY

Statements Involving Possibility

Examples:

> It is possible that the theory of evolution is false.
> The theory of evolution is perhaps false.
> It is not necessary that the theory of evolution is true.

Each of these statements is a modification, a sort of watering-down, of the statement "The theory of evolution is false." In general, statements involving possibility—and to assert that something is not necessarily true is equivalent to asserting that something is possibly false—say very little. In effect, they are statements that deny the impossibility of some event. All of the examples above are really asserting: "*It is not impossible that* the theory of evolution is false." In other words, it asserts that there is no contradiction involved in asserting the truth of the theory of evolution—in all, a very minimal assertion. In serious writing, such statements are only interesting when someone makes a claim that goes against what is generally held to be true. For instance, imagine a world-renowned evolutionary biologist asserting the possibility that the theory of evolution is false. Immediately, we would want to know why she thinks that is possible. Uttered by someone who is not an expert on evolution, the statement would be uninteresting.

Statements Involving Necessity

Examples:

> It is necessary that the theory of evolution is false.
> The theory of evolution must be false.
> The theory of evolution cannot be other than false.

Unlike statements involving possibility, statements involving necessity are very risky and say a great deal—usually too much. Here one wants to know not just why evolution is false, but why, since the statement is not a tautology, it is *necessary* that it is false. I have more to say about the modality of necessity below.

Statements Involving neither Possibility nor Necessity

Example:

> The theory of evolution is false.

On the one hand, this statement does not assert evolution *must be* false, so it says much less than a statement involving necessity. On the other hand, it is much more informative than a statement involving possibility. It takes a risk that a statement about possibility does not take.

ASSESSING ARGUMENTS WITH MODAL CONCLUSIONS

Possibility Statements

Here I give two examples of arguments with possibility/probability claims in the conclusions.

Studies show that consumption of moderate amounts of alcohol is strongly linked with prevention of heart disease.
So, consumption of moderate amounts of alcohol can be beneficial for health.

Pablito likes most spicy foods.
Burritos are spicy foods.
So, Pablito will probably like burritos.

In the first argument, the conclusion, as a statement about possibility, is very weak. Yet, given its weakness, the overall argument is strong, because a weak conclusion does not require much evidential support. Note also that the weak conclusion really does say much and is very interesting. Why? The view that consumption of alcohol in any amount is harmful has become so entrenched in modern thinking that studies that show moderate amounts of alcohol have healthful consequences seem startling. The conclusion here is very informative.

In the second argument, the conclusion is a statement about probability, not possibility. Still, it is weaker than "Pablito will like burritos." Being a weaker statement, the evidence of the premises makes the overall argument much stronger. Consider, in contrast, the conclusion "*It is possible that* Pablito will like burritos." That statement is so weak that the argument itself, though strong, is uninteresting.

In the main, statements involving possibility are very weak and uninteresting, except when one view is so entrenched that any alternative seems impossible or when pilot studies are done in science in an effort to establish the possibility of a link between two variables, like consumption of alcohol and improved health.

Necessity Claims

Examples:

Pablito likes most spicy foods.
Burritos are spicy foods.
So, it is necessary that Pablito will like burritos.

Pablito likes all spicy foods.
Burritos are spicy foods.
So, it is necessary that Pablito will like burritos.

In the first argument, the conclusion is a statement involving necessity and, thus, an extremely bold statement. Extremely bold statements require much evidence in support of them. The modality of necessity here makes for a weak argument.

In the second argument, with the first premise being universal, the argument is deductive, as the premises perfectly support the conclusion. In short, the truth of the premises necessarily makes the conclusion true, since the information in the conclusion is completely contained in the premises. So, prefacing the conclusion with "it is necessary that" here is redundant and unneeded.

Note, however, that people often use the modality of necessity in a rhetorically devious manner. Consider the following argument.

Plutarch was an historian that was concerned more with writing about people's virtue than writing about their history.
So, it must be true that Plutarch himself was a virtuous person.

Here we have a fallacy: The premise does not support the conclusion at all. Often people preface conclusions in this way in an effort to force you to accept a statement that is poorly supported by evidence. Be cautious of the modality of necessity. When it is used, it is often used wrongly and with intent to deceive.

Statements neither Possibility nor Necessity

Example:

Pablito likes most spicy foods.
Burritos are spicy foods.
So, Pablito will like burritos.

The conclusion involves neither possibility nor necessity, still it is a fairly bold statement and one that is given a reasonable amount of support by the premises.

Principle of Modality

Use the *Principle of Modality* as a useful tool in assessing the strength of arguments with modal conclusions.

ADDING THE MODALITY OF POSSIBILITY TO A CONCLUSION OF AN ARGUMENT WILL GENERALLY MAKE THE ARGUMENT STRONGER; ADDING THE MODALITY OF NECESSITY TO A CONCLUSION WILL GENERALLY MAKE IT WEAKER.

In the main, be suspicious of modal words or phrases in arguments. Statements involving necessity are tremendously risky and are mostly out of place in all arguing, except in formal philosophical works. Statements involving possibility are very weak and, for the most part, are only significant when such statements, stripped of the modality of possibility, are considered to be impossible.

MODULE 8
Conditions of Acceptance & Rejection

When to Accept an Argument

Module 5 gives the two conditions—the *Conditions of Acceptance*—that must be met before one is in a position to accept the conclusion of an argument as true. The first condition, CA_1, requires that each of the premises of an argument is true; the second condition, CA_2, requires that the premises, when *assumed* true, provide the right sort of support for the conclusion. To assure that those two conditions are met, ask yourself the following questions when analyzing an argument.

1) Are all the premises true?
2) Do the premises provide right type of support for conclusion?

Of course, it takes no special skills to answer the second question other than sober observation and a clear head. The difficulties come with the first question that concerns appropriateness. Thus, we shall be concerned almost exclusively with the first question.

To illustrate, I give four examples below of arguments, each decked out in Standard Argument Form. I then analyze each in turn.

Argument$_1$:

All philosophers are lovers of wisdom.
Aurelius is a philosopher.
So, Aurelius is a lover of wisdom.

Clearly, in this example, CA_1 is met. Both of the premises are true. Also, the premises provide the right kind of support—here absolute support—for the conclusion. So, CA_2 is met. The conclusion must be true.

Argument$_2$:

All fishwives are people that flout clowns.
All people that flout clowns are maudlin people.
So, all fishwives are maudlin people.

Here, of course, one should be suspicious because the conclusion is obviously false. Yet CA_2 is met, since the premises provide unconditional support for the conclusion. The problem is that both premises are patently false. Recall that only one premise needs to be false for us to be in position to reject the conclusion.

Argument$_3$:

All strongmen are natty scavengers.
All androids are natty scavengers.
So, all strongmen are androids.

The problem with this argument should be obvious. Even if the premises were true, the conclusion would not follow. There is something about the manner in which this argument is framed that makes us suspicious: All Hs are Ss; All As are Ss; so, All Hs are As. If each of two, potentially different categories has membership in a third, then the first must have membership in the second, which is absurd. That becomes more apparent, when we plug in different subject and predicate terms so that the premises are true.

Argument$_4$:

All Ginkgoes are trees.
All American Sycamores are trees.
So, all Ginkgoes are American Sycamores.

Here each of the premises is true, but the conclusion is still false, because the premises, when taken together, offer no evidence for the conclusion. One could readily accept both as true—and here one must—yet be justified in not accepting the conclusion. When CA_2 is met, the truth of the premises warrants acceptance of the conclusion as true.

When to Reject an Argument

In the prior section, we answered the question of when to accept the conclusion of an argument as true by giving two conditions that must be met. We called them the *Conditions of Acceptance* in module 5. To answer the question of when *not* to accept the conclusion of an argument as true, I turn to the *Conditions of Rejection*.

CR_1: THE ARGUMENT WILL HAVE AT LEAST ONE FALSE PREMISE.
CR_2: THE PREMISES WILL PROVIDE LITTLE OR NO SUPPORT FOR CONCLUSION.

THREE WAYS PREMISES CAN SUPPORT A CONCLUSION

Each of the following three examples are given to illustrate the different sorts of support that premises can give to a conclusion, independently of the actual truth or untruth of the premises.

Deductively Valid Argument

THE PREMISES, IF TRUE, PROVIDE *INCONTROVERTIBLE SUPPORT* FOR THE CONCLUSION.

Example:

> All the limes in the aubergine bowl are ripe.
> Filbert took a lime from the aubergine bowl.
> So, Filbert took a ripe lime.

In a deductively valid argument, the premises completely support the conclusion. If they are true, the conclusion must be true as well. Deductive validity is an all-or-nothing affair: The premises either fully support the conclusion or they fail to do so. When the second condition is met and the premises are true, we have the perfect sort of argument—what is commonly called a "sound" argument.

Inductively Strong Argument

THE PREMISES, IF TRUE, PROVIDE A *REASONABLE DEGREE OF SUPPORT* FOR THE CONCLUSION.

Example:

> Most of the limes in the aubergine bowl are ripe.
> Filbert took a lime from the aubergine bowl.
> So, Filbert took a ripe lime.

In an inductively strong argument, the premises, assumed true, give one at least more reason than not to think that conclusion will be true. When they are true, the conclusion will probably true be as well. In contrast to deductive validity, which is an all-or-nothing affair, inductive strength is a matter of degrees. The premises give us more reason to accept, rather than reject, the conclusion. When the second condition is met and the premises are true, we have what is commonly called a "cogent" argument.

Fallacy

THE PREMISES, IF TRUE, PROVIDE *LITTLE OR NO SUPPORT* FOR THE CONCLUSION.

Examples:

> Few of the limes in the aubergine bowl are ripe.
> Filbert took a lime from the aubergine bowl.
> So, Filbert took a ripe lime.

All of the limes in the aubergine bowl are ripe.
Filbert took a ripe lime.
So, Filbert took a lime from the aubergine bowl.

The first is an example of an inductive argument that is not strong—i.e., its premises do not give us more reason to accept, rather than reject, the conclusion. Here the premises give little support for the conclusion. The conclusion may in fact be true, but we would not be rationally justified in believing it so because the premises, if true, provide little support for the conclusion.

The second is an example of a deductive argument that is not valid. It seems clear that the author of this argument intends that the conclusion follow necessarily from the premises. However, even if we grant the truth of the premises, the conclusion does not necessarily follow. Though the conclusion may in fact be true, we would not be rationally justified in believing it so because the premises, if true, do not provide incontrovertible support for the conclusion. Filbert could have taken an oatmeal cookie from a plastic bag.

In sum, we have a fallacy whenever we have a deductive argument that is not valid or an inductive argument that is not strong.

MODULE 9
Three Common Deductive Arguments

This module looks at three types of deductive arguments and one fallacious form of each type. Remember that for deductive arguments the support given by the premises is absolute (Module 8). The right sort of deductive argument, one that is valid, has premises that, if true, make necessary the truth of the conclusion.

MODUS PONENS (AFFIRMING THE ANTECEDENT)

MODUS PONENS, MEANING "THE AFFIRMING WAY," IS A VALID DEDUCTIVE ARGUMENT WITH THREE STATEMENTS: A CONDITIONAL PREMISE, A PREMISE THAT AFFIRMS THE ANTECEDENT OF THE CONDITIONAL PREMISE, AND A CONCLUSION THAT AFFIRMS THE CONSEQUENT OF THE CONDITIONAL PREMISE.

It has the following form:

If α, then β.
α.
So, β.

Examples:

(1) <u>You [Xeniades] must obey me [Diogenes the Cynic]</u>, although (2) I am your slave; (for.) (3) if a physician or a steersman were in slavery, he would be obeyed. (Diogenes Laertius, *Lives* VI.2)

(1) Now you saw that I believe in spiritual things.... But (2) if I believe in spiritual things, I must quite inevitably believe in spirits. (Plato, *Apology*)

The first argument comprises two simple statements and a conditional. The conditional statement is to be taken counterfactually. Its antecedent is false, but its counterfactual force is such that, if the antecedent *were* true, it would be sufficient to generate the truth of the conclusion. In Standard Argument Form:

If a physician or a steersman were in slavery, he would be obeyed.
Diogenes is a slave [and is like a physician or steersman].
So, Diogenes should be obeyed.

In the second argument, there are only two statements—a simple statement and a conditional—neither of which is the conclusion. The conclusion is left unexpressed, but is implicitly understood as the consequent of statement two, "I must believe in spirits." In Standard Argument Form:

If Socrates believes in spiritual things, then he must believe in spirits.
Socrates believes in spiritual things.
[So, Socrates believes in spirits].

Let us now consider an invalid argument form, where the consequent, not the antecedent, is affirmed.

If α, then β.
β.
So, α.

Here premise one tells us that the truth of α is sufficient to generate the truth of β. Premise two tells us that that β is true. But since β is not sufficient to generate α, we cannot be certain that α is true, given the truth of both premises. This deductive argument is formally distinct from modens ponens and invalid, as the premises poorly support the conclusion. To see that unmistakably, let us consider the following argument about pahoehoe—a type of smooth, solid lava.

If Jane studies pahoehoe, she studies lava.
Jane studies lava.
So, Jane studies pahoehoe.

Here the first premise is true, but the conclusion does not follow on assumption of the truth of the second premise.

MODUS TOLLENS (DENYING THE CONSEQUENT)

MODUS TOLLENS, MEANING "THE DENYING WAY," IS A VALID DEDUCTIVE ARGUMENT WITH THREE STATEMENTS: A CONDITIONAL PREMISE, A PREMISE THAT DENIES THE CONSEQUENT OF THE CONDITIONAL PREMISE, AND A CONCLUSION THAT AFFIRMS THE DENIAL OF THE ANTECEDENT OF THE CONDITIONAL PREMISE.

It has the following form:

If α, then β.
Not β.
So, not α.

Example:

Let it be said at once then, that (1) if the bodies of the stars moved in a quantity either of air or of fire diffused throughout the whole, ~~as everyone assumes them to do,~~ the noise which they created would inevitably be tremendous and ... would reach and shatter things here on earth. (Since) (2) that obviously does not happen, (3) their motions cannot in any instance be due either to soul or to external violence. (Aristotle, *On the Heavens*)

In Standard Argument Form:

> If the bodies of the stars moved in a quantity either of air or of fire diffused throughout the whole, the noise which they created would inevitably be tremendous and ... would reach and shatter things here on earth.
> It is not the case that the noise is tremendous and that it reaches and shatters things here on earth.
> So, their motions cannot in any instance be due either to soul or to external violence.

Let us now consider an invalid form where the antecedent is denied.

If α, then β.
Not α.
So, not β.

Again premise one tells us that the truth of α is sufficient to generate the truth of β. Premise two tells us that that α is not true. But since the denial of α is not sufficient to generate the denial of β, we cannot be sure that not-β is true. This argument is formally distinct from modens tollens and invalid, as its premises poorly support the conclusion. To see that plainly, consider again another argument about pahoehoe.

> If Jane studies pahoehoe, she studies lava.
> Jane does not study pahoehoe.
> So, Jane does not study lava.

Here premise one is true, but the conclusion does not follow, because premise two, assumed true, does not work with premise one to guarantee the truth of the conclusion. For instance, Jane could be studying a type of lava that is not pahoehoe.

DISJUNCTIVE SYLLOGISM

DISJUNCTIVE SYLLOGISM IS A VALID DEDUCTIVE ARGUMENT WITH THREE STATEMENTS: A DISJUNCTIVE PREMISE, A PREMISE THAT DENIES ALL BUT ONE OF THE DISJUNCTIVE STATEMENTS, AND A CONCLUSION THAT AFFIRMS THE ONE REMAINING DISJUNCTIVE STATEMENT THAT HAS NOT BEEN DENIED.

It has the following form:

α, β, or γ.
Not α and not β.
So, γ.

Here there are no limits to the number of disjuncts in the first statement: There can be two, twenty-two, or even two hundred and twenty-two. It is only necessary that the second statement deny all but one of them for the argument to go through. I give two examples, each from Aristotle's *Nicomachean Ethics*.

(1) The states of the soul by which we always grasp the truth and never make mistakes, about what can or cannot be otherwise, are scientific knowledge, practical wisdom, wisdom, and intuition. (2) None of the first three—practical wisdom, scientific knowledge, wisdom—is possible about origins. (3) <u>The remaining possibility is that we have intuition about origins</u>.

Since (1) there are three conditions arising in the soul—feelings, capacities and states—(2) virtue must be one of these.... First, (3) neither virtues nor vices are feelings.... (4) [T]he virtues are not capacities either.... (5) If <u>the virtues are neither feelings nor capacities, they are states</u>.

In the first example, the first statement lists three states of the soul that enable us to grasp truth unerringly. The second rules out all but the third as options. The fourth, then, is the conclusion. In Standard Argument Form:

Scientific knowledge, practical wisdom, wisdom, and intuition are the states of the soul by which we always unerringly grasp the truth about what can and cannot be otherwise.
Scientific knowledge, practical wisdom, and wisdom give us no truth about origins.
So, intuition gives us truth about origins.

In the second example, the first proposition is irrelevant, so do not include it in your reconstruction. Statement one generates statement two, which gets the disjunctive syllogism rolling. We can rewrite statement two as "Virtue must be a feeling, capacity, or state." Statement five is obviously the conclusion here, but it's not quite what we want, since it's in conditionalized form. However, we can rewrite it as the statement "The virtues are states," given the eliminative work of statement three. In Standard Argument Form:

There are three conditions arising in the soul—feelings, capacities and states.
So, virtues must be feelings, capacities, or states.
Neither virtues nor vices are feelings.
The virtues are not capacities either.
So, [the virtues are states.].

Let us now consider an invalid form that looks valid, but is certainly not.

α or β.
α.
Not β.

The first premise asserts that α or β is true, or both. The second premise asserts that α is true. The truth of α, however, gives us no certainty that β is false, since the truth of both statements is consistent with the denial of the truth of the conclusion, not "not β," which is equivalent to β. Therefore, since the truth of the premises does not guarantee the truth of the conclusion, the argument is invalid. One can demonstrate easily the invalidity by giving an argument in which the first premise has the inclusive sense of "or"—i.e., a sense in which both disjuncts can be true.

Amartya or Yuri took a trip to Kamchatka.
Amartya took a trip to Kamchatka.
So, Yuri did not take a trip to Kamchatka.

Plainly the sense of "or" in premise one is *inclusive*. There is no reason to think, unless one is given evidence to the contrary, that Amartya's trip to Kamchatka rules out Yuri's trip to Kamchatka.

There is an *exclusive* sense of "or"—meaning "one or the other, but not both"—in which the argument does go through. Consider this argument.

Blaine was dealt a club or a spade.
Blaine was dealt a club.
So, Blaine was not dealt a spade.

The difficulty is that "or" has both senses in English and, given that, one cannot assume exclusivity. So, this form of argument is invalid.

MODULE 10
Common Inductive Arguments

This module looks at three main types of inductive arguments: analogical argument, statistical syllogism, and inductive generalization. Remember that for inductive arguments the support given by the premises is a matter of degrees (Module 8). The right sort of inductive argument, one that it strong, has premises that, if true, give one more reason than not to think that the conclusion too will be true. Strength varies, then, in proportion to the evidence given on behalf of a conclusion.

ANALOGICAL ARGUMENT

AN *ANALOGICAL ARGUMENT* IS AN ARGUMENT THAT DRAWS A CONCLUSION ABOUT ONE THING—WHETHER A PARTICULAR THING OR A CLASS OF THINGS—BASED ON THE SIMILARITIES IT HAS WITH ANOTHER THING.

The overall strength of such arguments is generally difficult to assess. Much rides on the relevance of what is predicated of the things being compared.

Let us begin with an example:

High-hearted son of Tydeus, why ask of my generation? As is the generation of leaves, so is that of humanity. The wind scatters the leaves on the ground, but the live timber burgeons with leaves again in the season of spring returning. So one generation of men will grow while another dies (Homer, *Iliad* VI).

Following the guidelines for Standard Argument Form in Module 6, we flesh out the argument as follows:

The generations of leaves are like the generations of men.
The wind scatters the leaves to the ground, but the live timber sends forth
    new leaves in the season of spring.
So, one generation of men grow while another dies.

Here the first premise is a statement of comparison with nothing specific being compared—i.e., there are no attributes given. Still premises one and two do seem to give sufficient grounds for thinking the conclusion to be more likely to be true than false. The example can be formally presented as follows:

P is similar to Q.
P has attribute α.
So, Q has attribute α.

Notice that premise one, irrespective of what items or categories are put in the place of P or Q, is unhelpfully vague. It tells us that P is similar to Q, but it does not tell us how it is similar to Q. Thus, premise one tells us almost nothing about the two items or categories, so it is generally impossible to assess.

Analogical arguments are better expressed more fully as follows:

P has attributes α, β, and γ.
Q has attributes α, β, and γ.
P has attribute δ.
So, Q has attribute δ.

Here the statement "P is similar to Q" is stated more precisely in the first two premises, where the similarities are spelled out by specific attributes α, β, and γ. Of course, the number of things predicated in any of the statements can vary.

Example:

Just as a sailor is one of a number of members of a community, so, we say, is a citizen. And though sailors differ in their capacities (for one is an oarsman, another a captain, another a lookout, and others have other sorts of titles) it is clear both that the most exact account of the virtue of each sort of sailor will be peculiar to him, and similarly that there will also be some common account that fits them all. For the safety of the voyage is a task of all of them, since this is what each of the sailors strives for. In the same way, then, the citizens too, even though they are dissimilar, have the safety of the community as their task (Aristotle *Politics* III.4)

Put into Standard Argument Form:

A sailor is a member of a ship.
A citizen is a member of a community.
There is a different account of virtue (i.e., different function) for each sort of sailor.
There is a different account of virtue (i.e., different function) for each sort of citizen.
Yet there is some common account of virtue for each sailor (i.e., the security of the ship).
So, likewise, there must be some common account of virtue for each citizen (i.e., the security of the city).

Premises one and two are obvious enough. Assessment of the strength of this argument hinges on a critical evaluation of premises three through five.

Here are two standards of strength to help evaluate the strength of analogical arguments:

RELEVANCE CONDITION: THE THINGS PREDICATED OF THE SUBJECT TERMS (P AND Q) IN THE FIRST TWO PREMISES (α, β, AND γ) MUST BE RELEVANT TO THE THING OR THINGS PREDICATED IN THE THIRD PREMISE AND CONCLUSION (δ). P AND Q HAVING α, β, AND γ AND P HAVING δ MUST BE GOOD REASONS TO CONVINCE ANYONE THAT Q TOO MUST HAVE δ.

IRRELEVANCE CONDITION: THERE MUST BE A LACK OF STRIKING DISSIMILARITIES BETWEEN P AND Q. FOR INSTANCE, P MAY HAVE ATTRIBUTES ϵ, ζ, η, AND θ THAT Q DOES NOT HAVE, AND THEY COULD BE RELEVANT AND GOOD REASONS FOR Q NOT HAVING δ.

Overall, I believe that analogical arguments in philosophy are misleading and seldom make for strong arguments. Since philosophy is about clarity, they generally do more to obfuscate than clarify what one is attempting to say.

STATISTICAL SYLLOGISM

A *STATISTICAL SYLLOGISM* IS AN ARGUMENT WITH TWO PREMISES—ONE OF WHICH IS A STATISTICAL STATEMENT THAT CONCERNS A SUBJECT (I.E., "X% OF PS," "FEW PS,", OR "MOST PS") OF WHICH SOMETHING IS PREDICATED (I.E., α) AND THE OTHER OF WHICH IS A PARTICULAR STATEMENT—AND A PARTICULAR CONCLUSION.

The general form of a statistical syllogism may be expressed thus:

X % of all Ps have α.
W is a P.
So, *W* has α.

In assessing statistical syllogisms, roughly anything over 50% in premise one will make a strong argument. At least, anything over 50% will afford us more reason to think that the conclusion is true rather than false.
Examples:

12% of the prospective job applicants are college-educated.
Oblomov is a prospective job applicant.
So, Oblomov is not college-educated.

82% of kitchens are rooms redolent of garlic or onion.
This room is my kitchen.
So, this room is a room redolent of garlic or onion.

In the first argument, notice that the first premise is a weak statement, but the argument is strong because the conclusion is the denial of the statement, "Oblomov is college educated." In asserting that 12% of the job applicants are college-educated, premise one is also stating "88% of the prospective job applicants are *not* college educated." It should be obvious why the second argument is strong.

Here are two standards of strength for statistical syllogisms.

STRENGTH CONDITION: STRENGTH IS ASCERTAINED BY PREMISE ONE'S PROXIMITY TO 100% (I.E., THE CLOSER TO 100%, THE STRONGER THE ARGUMENT) OR 0% (I.E., THE CLOSER TO 0%, THE WEAKER THE ARGUMENT).

AVAILABLE-EVIDENCE CONDITION: ONE MUST USE ALL THE AVAILABLE EVIDENCE IN CONSTRUCTING OR ASSESSING SUCH AN ARGUMENT.

When condition two is not met, we have the *Fallacy of Incomplete Evidence*.

THE *FALLACY OF INCOMPLETE EVIDENCE* OCCURS WHEN ALL OF THE AVAILABLE EVIDENCE IS NOT USED IN AN INDUCTIVE ARGUMENT.

Example:

98% of the attendants at the lush Hollywood bash are teetotalers.
W.C. Fields is an attendant.
So, W.C. Fields is a teetotaler.

Those of us who remember W.C. Fields know well that he was very fond of imbibing alcohol. The argument, as given, commits the *fallacy of incomplete evidence*. Yet, it can be revised as follows and made strong, if we, using all the available evidence, rewrite the argument.

98% of the attendants at the lush Hollywood bash are teetotalers.
W.C. Fields is an attendant.
W.C. Fields is a noted imbiber of strong spirits.
So, W.C. Fields is *not* a teetotaler.

As is characteristic of all inductive arguments, additional information (i.e., "W.C. Fields is a noted imbiber of strong spirits") added to an argument that strongly supports "W.C. Fields is a teetotaler" winds up strongly supporting the contradictory statement, "W.C. Fields is not a teetotaler."

Types of Statistical Syllogism

Argument from Authority

Here is the general form of the argument from authority:

> Most of what authority *A* says about some topic P is true.
> *A* says α about P.
> So, α is true.

Assume premise one is true only when the following conditions are met:

EXPERTISE CONDITION: THE AUTHORITY MUST BE EXPERT IN THE AREA ABOUT WHICH HE SPEAKS.
CONSENSUS CONDITION: THERE MUST BE GENERAL AGREEMENT AMONG EXPERTS IN THAT AREA.
CONSISTENCY CONDITION: THE AUTHORITY MUST BE IN AGREEMENT WITH THE MAJORITY OF OTHER EXPERTS.

When each of these conditions is met, we have good reason to accept the first premise as true. Otherwise, we have the *Fallacious Argument from Authority*.

THE *FALLACIOUS ARGUMENT FROM AUTHORITY* OCCURS WHEN ANY OF THE THREE CONDITIONS LISTED ABOVE IS NOT MET.

Be on your guard for arguments that look like compelling appeals to authority that are poorly constructed. The following is an example.

> Physicians are experts on medicines.
> Most physicians give Zoon Aspirin to their patients more than any other brand.
> So, Zoon Aspirin is better than all other brands.

In the main, aspirin is aspirin, and often the reason one brand is preferred by physicians over others is that they can get it at a discounted price. Here the conclusion does not follow, because premise two does not say that most physicians acknowledge that Zoon Aspirin *is* better than all other brands; it says only that most physicians give it to their patients.

Argument against the Man

Here is the general form of the argument against the man:

> Most of what someone *S* says about some topic P is false.
> *S* says α about P.

So, α is false.

This argument, of course, is strong, not fallacious, given the assumed truth of the premises, but in general we will seldom be in a position to accept the first premise as true, for there is a general inclination in people not to talk about things concerning of which they are ignorant. So be chary and suspicious, when you come across such an argument. It is probable that premise one will be justified by nothing other than personal dislike.

Argument from Consensus

Here is the general form of the argument from consensus:

> Most of what the majority of people say about any topic P is true.
> The majority of people say α.
> So, α is true.

Example:

> Most Americans believe that angels exist.
> So, angels exist.

The problem with this argument is obvious. As Plato constantly reminded his readers, the majority is seldom, if ever, in a position to be experts on any issue. Arguments of this type, however, are useful when consensus, not truth, is at stake. We might, for example, want to decide whether or not taxes should be raised and so we appeal to a consensus of opinion.

INDUCTIVE GENERALIZATION

AN *INDUCTIVE GENERALIZATION* IS A TYPE OF INDUCTIVE ARGUMENT THAT GOES FROM PARTICULAR PREMISES TO A GENERALIZED CONCLUSION.

Example (in Standard Argument Form):

> $Chimp_1$ is capable of mastering certain linguistic signs.
> $Chimp_2$ is capable of mastering certain linguistic signs.
>
>   .   .   .
>
> $Chimp_n$ is capable of mastering certain linguistic signs.
> So, all chimps are capable of mastering certain linguistic signs.

Let us simplify the example above by collapsing the premises into one:

> Number "n" of *observed* chimps are capable of mastering certain linguistic signs.

So, *all* chimps are capable of mastering certain linguistic signs.

Let us next add another example:

> *50% of the time* I've taken a philosophy class I've gotten a 'D.'
> So, *50% of all* the philosophy classes I'll ever take I'll get a 'D.'

Unlike the first example, which has a universal generalization as a conclusion, the second has a statistical generalization as one. We can represent both by the following general form:

> X% of *observed* Ps have α.
> So, X% of *all* Ps have α (where X may be 100%).

How will you know when to accept the conclusion of such an argument as true? For instance, both of the examples above do not seem strong. Why not?

Here we must appeal to two standards of strength for inductive generalizations—variation and size.

VARIATION STANDARD: THE SAMPLE IN THE PREMISE MUST BE SUFFICIENTLY VARIED.
SIZE STANDARD: THE SAMPLE IN THE PREMISE MUST BE SUFFICIENTLY LARGE.

To ensure variety, a *random sample* should be taken from a population. That guarantees, insofar as that is possible, each member of population has an equal chance of being selected. On the issue of size, we may say this: The larger the sample, the surer we can be that the sample closely resembles the population.

Fallacies Related to Inductive Generalizations

Hasty Generalization

A *HASTY GENERALIZATION* IS AN INDUCTIVE GENERALIZATION WHOSE SAMPLE SIZE IS TOO SMALL TO SECURE THE TRUTH OF THE CONCLUSION.

Example:

Madame Luna predicted in 1980 the fall of Russian communism.
So, Madame Luna is a reputable psychic.

To see why this argument is not strong, let us revise it as follows.

One observed prediction of Madame Luna has come true.
So, all of Madame Luna's predictions must be true.

Here assessment of Luna's psychic abilities actually rests on a judgment based on one instance. It fails also to take into consideration any failed predictions or any other successes—i.e., it violates the available-evidence condition.

Biased Sample

A *BIASED SAMPLE* IS AN INDUCTIVE GENERALIZATION WHOSE SAMPLE LACKS SUFFICIENT VARIATION TO GUARANTEE THE TRUTH OF THE CONCLUSION.

Example:

70% of the 200 people that I interviewed at the new food gallery in the library thought that the money to build it was well spent.
So, 70% of all people think that the money for the library's new food gallery was money well spent.

The difficulty occurs because the interviewing occurred *only* at the food gallery. One would fully expect that people eating there would likely approve of it.

MODULE 11
Common Fallacies

Module 9 lists three common types of deductive arguments—modus ponens, modus tollens, and disjunctive syllogism—along with a corresponding fallacious form for each type. Module 10 lists three of the most common inductive arguments—analogical argument, statistical syllogism, and inductive generalization—as well as certain related inductive fallacies.

This module begins with a more generic definition of "fallacy" than the one given at the end of Module 5 and then gives some of the most frequently encountered fallacies. While reading, try to explain why each of the examples listed below is an instance of the type of fallacy described or defined.

WHAT IS A FALLACY?

As we have seen in Module 5, arguments aim to demonstrate the truth of a certain claim, the conclusion, by putting forth at least one other claim as evidence or a reason for it. Arguments can be valid, when the premise(s), supposed true, absolutely supports the conclusion. They can also be strong, when the premise(s), supposed true, give a reasonable degree of support for the conclusion. When an argument fails to be valid or strong, it is a fallacy.

A *FALLACY* IS A MISTAKE IN REASONING THAT OCCURS WHEN THE PREMISE(S) OF AN ARGUMENT, ASSUMED TRUE, FAIL TO SUPPORT THE CONCLUSION.

Note that fallacies have nothing to do with the falsity of the premise(s).

Some of the fallacies listed below have been mentioned earlier as well.

FALLACIES OF RELEVANCE

Accident

THE *ARGUMENT FROM ACCIDENT* OCCURS WHEN ONE APPLIES A GENERAL RULE TO A PARTICULAR INSTANCE THAT IT WAS NOT MEANT TO COVER.

Example:

Excessive noise in public places is generally frowned upon, so you should not cheer at the hockey game when the Detroit Red Wings score a goal.

Appeal to Force

THE *ARGUMENT FROM FORCE* IS REASONING THAT APPEALS TO FORCE, NOT EVIDENCE, AS A MEANS OF PERSUASION.

Example:

CEO Milovich's belief that there ought to be absolutely no government intervention in the practice of businesses must be correct. He is, after all, my boss and those persons who have expressed the slightest disagreement with him on political matters have always been fired.

Appeal to Pity

THE *ARGUMENT FROM PITY* IS AN APPEAL TO PITY IN ORDER TO HAVE SOME STATEMENT ACCEPTED AS TRUE.

Example:

You've got to give me at least a "B" in Logic, because I'll lose my scholarship if you don't and I can't continue on with my education without my scholarship.

Unfortunately, this argument is increasingly used by students these days, without the least concern that asking for and being given a grade that they have not earned is wanton.

Missing the Point

MISSING THE POINT OCCURS WHEN THE EVIDENCE IN THE PREMISES OF AN ARGUMENT LEADS TO A CONCLUSION OTHER THAN THE ONE GIVEN.

Example:

Downs-syndrome children cannot experience many of the enjoyments that other children can, thus all Downs-syndrome foetuses ought to be aborted.

Red Herring

A RED HERRING HAPPENS WHEN YOU IGNORE SOME POINT OF AN ARGUMENT BY DIVERTING ATTENTION TO ANOTHER ISSUE.

Example:

Gunderpugg believes in the right to own a gun, but he doesn't believe in hunting. So, Gunderpugg doesn't really believe in the right to own a gun.

Here one may believe in the right to own a gun, for self-protection, and not believe in hunting, say, because of a certain ethical stance.

Straw Man

A *STRAW MAN* OCCURS WHEN YOU PRESENT A PERSON'S ARGUMENT IN A WEAK FORM IN ORDER TO REFUTE IT READILY.

Example:

Freudian psychoanalysis is patently absurd. No one can trust a scientist who gets inspiration from mythology.

Here the issue is not the source of Freud's inspiration (i.e., the myth of Oedipus), but whether or not his theory of psychoanalysis, based on the Oedipus complex, is correct. Scientists draw inspiration from strange sources.

STATISTICAL FALLACIES AND MORE FALLACIES OF WEAK INDUCTION

Appeal to Ignorance

THE *APPEAL TO IGNORANCE* OCCURS WHEN YOU ARGUE FALLACIOUSLY THAT SOMETHING IS TRUE (OR FALSE) BECAUSE NO ONE HAS PROVEN IT FALSE (OR TRUE).

Example:

No one has shown that there is no intelligent life on other planets, so life must exist on another planet somewhere.

Lack of evidence for some statement is not evidence for its denial. Lack of evidence for some statement is just lack of evidence and it cannot be used as evidence for the contradictory statement of that claim. In general, when it comes to existence claims, it is reasonable for the burden of proof to be on the person asserting the existence of something, say aliens from another planet, since belief in the non-existence, when evidence for existence is wanting, is simply economical.

Biased Sample

THE *ARGUMENT FROM BIASED SAMPLE* HAPPENS WHEN A GENERAL STATEMENT IS GIVEN SUPPORT BY AN UNVARIED SAMPLE (SEE ALSO MODULE 10).

Example:

> 78% of all the students interviewed at Colby College endorsed the democratic candidate, so 78% of all people in Maine endorse the democratic candidate.

Hasty Generalization

A *HASTY GENERALIZATION* OCCURS WHEN THERE IS AN INADEQUATE AMOUNT OF EVIDENCE TO GROUND A GENERAL STATEMENT (SEE ALSO MODULE 10).

Example:

> Each of the three introductory courses I've taken at the University of Michigan was difficult. It must be the case that every introductory course offered at the University of Michigan is difficult.

Slippery Slope

A *SLIPPERY-SLOPE* HAPPENS WHEN A CHAIN REACTION, SUGGESTED BY THE PREMISES, IS NOT RATIONALLY JUSTIFIED BY THE PREMISES.

Example:

> Belgian beers are being imported to America at a rate that is 500% greater than that of 10 years ago. It follows that in 10 more years, everyone in America will be drinking Belgian beers.

CAUSAL FALLACIES

Gambler's Fallacy

THE GAMBLER'S FALLACY HAPPENS WHEN TWO INDEPENDENT EVENTS (I.E., EVENTS THAT HAVE NO IMPACT ON EACH OTHER) ARE SEEN TO BE DEPENDENT.

Example:

> Aristidis won money each of the last three times he's played the slots at Greektown Casino, so he'll win money when he plays slots tomorrow.

Slots, at casinos, are mathematically arranged, on average, to give players some percentage of what they put into the machine on each play. Aristidis' win streak is better attributed to chance than to any such skill he might be thought to possess with slots.

Genetic Fallacy

THE *GENETIC FALLACY* HAPPENS WHEN THE ORIGIN OF SOME STATEMENT IS TAKEN TO BE EVIDENCE FOR IT.

Example:

> Petrusha believes that deity exists, because she was told so when she was young.

Here Petrusha's being told when young that deity exists explains how she has come to believe that God exists, but it is not any sort of evidence on behalf of the existence of God that any rational person would embrace.

Ignoring a Common Cause

IGNORING A COMMON CAUSE AMOUNTS TO ATTRIBUTING FALSELY ONE OF THE EFFECTS OF A CAUSE AS A CAUSE FOR ANOTHER OF THE EFFECTS OF THE SAME (UNDISCLOSED) CAUSE.

Example:

> When the days get shorter and the nights get longer in Canada, the temperature there drops. Consequently, the shortness of each day is the cause of the drop in temperature.

It is the path and inclination of the sun during winter that is the cause of both the shortness of days and the drop in temperature in Canada.

Post Hoc (ergo Propter Hoc)

THE *POST-HOC FALLACY* OCCURS WHEN CAUSAL FORCE IS ATTRIBUTED TO SOME EVENT SIMPLY BECAUSE IT OCCURRED PRIOR TO SOME OTHER EVENT.

Example:

> When Amiere helped a blind person to cross the street the other day, she found a fifty-dollar bill on the other side of the street. So, kindness pays.

OTHER FALLACIES

Amphiboly

AMPHIBOLY HAPPENS WHEN AN ARGUMENT CONTAINS AT LEAST ONE SYNTACTICALLY AMBIGUOUS STATEMENT.

Example:

> Rhonda told to Rhenny that she had the necklace. So, Rhenny had the neck-
> lace.

Here "she" in the premise does not specifically pick out Rhonda or Rhenny.

Begging the Question

BEGGING THE QUESTION HAPPENS WHEN A CONCLUSION IS DRAWN FROM
PREMISES THAT ARE THEMSELVES SUSPICIOUS AND IN NEED OF JUSTIFICATION.

Example:

> Everything has some cause, so the cosmos too must have a cause.

Composition

THE *FALLACY OF COMPOSITION* OCCURS WHEN WHAT IS TRUE OF SOMETHING'S
PARTS IS TAKEN TO BE TRUE OF IT AS A WHOLE.

Example:

> Each of the several items I've placed on the pizza is toothsome, so the pizza
> itself will be toothsome.

Imagine a pizza with chocolate-covered cherries, brine-soaked bran, whitefish,
black-patent malt, molasses, goat tripe, and artichokes. It seems that such a pizza
would likely be a gourmand's nightmare, even if the gourmand found each of the
items, considered separately, toothsome.

Division

THE *FALLACY OF DIVISION* OCCURS WHEN YOU ARGUE THAT WHAT IS TRUE OF
SOMETHING'S WHOLE IS TAKEN TO BE TRUE OF ITS PARTS.

Example:

> The community of Birmingham is rich, so each of its citizens is rich.

Equivocation

THE *FALLACY OF EQUIVOCATION* IS AN ARGUMENT WHERE A WORD IS USED IN ONE
SENSE IN ONE PART OF AN ARGUMENT AND IN ANOTHER SENSE IN ANOTHER PART.

Example:

> Chapter 21 is the end of the book. The end of everything is some good thing. Therefore, the chapter 21 will be good.

False Dichotomy

THE *FALLACY OF FALSE DICHOTOMY* OCCURS WHEN A CONCLUSION IS SUPPORTED BY A DISJUNCTIVE PREMISE WHOSE TRUTH IS SUSPECT (I.E., THE DISJUNCTIVE STATEMENT IS NOT EXCLUSIVE OR EXHAUSTIVE).

Example:

> Garriston Fluffs eats spare ribs or white asparagus each day. Since Fluffs is eating white asparagus today, he will not be eating ribs.

The first premise allows for the possibility that Fluffs eats both each day.

SECTION C
Reconstruction through Diagramming

MODULE 12
Fundamentals of Diagramming

Arguments, as we shall see in this and the next module, can be relatively short and simple, comprising one or a few premises and a conclusion, or lengthy and complex, where the argument as a whole comprises numerous other arguments as parts. The simplest argument is a conclusion with one premise. Complex arguments can be indefinitely large. Darwin's *Origin of Species,* for instance, can be taken as one long and large argument to show that species are not fixed.

Since arguments can be so complex, they cannot be analyzed adequately before they are completely and correctly reconstructed. Thus, diagramming them is extraordinarily helpful. Diagramming gives you, as a critical reasoner, the opportunity to see the argument as a whole and how the various parts fit together to form the whole. Once the diagram is completed, you are in position to begin evaluation by assessing the various evidential links of the parts.

TWO TYPES OF ARGUMENT

Simple Arguments

A *SIMPLE ARGUMENT* IS ONE THAT HAS ONLY ONE EVIDENTIAL LINK—I.E., ONE ARROW.

Examples:

Sandeep loves to travel, for he has a brand new set of suitcases in his basement.

Sandeep loves to travel. He does so often and what he does often he loves.

Analyses:

(1) Sandeep loves to travel, (for)(2) he has a brand new set of suitcases in his basement.

(1) Sandeep loves to travel. (2) He does so often and (3) what he does often he loves.

The first is diagrammed below, at left, the second is diagrammed below, at right.

COMPOUND ARGUMENTS

A *COMPOUND ARGUMENT* IS AN ARGUMENT WITH MORE THAN ONE EVIDENTIAL LINK—I.E., MORE THAN ONE ARROW.

I give two illustrations below. Each is fairly tough and lengthy, though they serve the purpose of illustration well, as arguments are often tough and lengthy.

> Self-interest, or rather self-love, or *egoism*, has been more plausibly substituted as the basis of morality. But I consider our relations with others as constituting the boundaries of morality. With ourselves, we stand on the ground of identity, not of relation, which last, requiring two subjects, excludes self-love confined to a single one. To ourselves, in strict language, we can owe no duties, obligation requiring also two parties. Self-love, therefore, is no part of morality. (Thomas Jefferson to Thomas Law, 1814)

> As we continually see that organisms of all kinds are rendered in some degree sterile from their constitutions having been disturbed by slightly different and new conditions of life, we need not feel surprise at hybrids being in some degree sterile, for their constitutions can hardly fail to have been disturbed from being compounded of two distinct organisations. This parallelism is supported by another parallel, but directly opposite, class of facts; namely, that the vigour and fertility of all organic beings are increased by slight changes in their conditions of life, and that the offspring of slightly modified forms or varieties acquire from being crossed increased vigour and fertility. So that, on the one hand, considerable changes in the conditions of life and crosses between greatly modified forms, lessen fertility; and on the other hand, lesser changes in the conditions of life and crosses between less modified forms, increase fertility. (Charles Darwin, *Origin of Species*)

Analyses:

(1) ~~Self-interest, or rather self-love, or *egoism*, has been more plausibly substituted as the basis of morality~~. But (2) I consider our relations with others as constituting the boundaries of morality. (3) With ourselves, we stand on the ground of identity, not of relation, which last, requiring two subjects, excludes self-love confined to a single one. (4) To ourselves, in strict lan-

guage, we can owe no duties, obligation requiring also two parties. (5) <u>Self-love, therefore, is no part of morality.</u>

As we continually see that (1) organisms of all kinds are rendered in some degree sterile from their constitutions having been disturbed by slightly different and new conditions of life, ~~we need not feel surprise at~~ (2) hybrids being in some degree sterile, for (3) their constitutions can hardly fail to have been disturbed from being compounded of two distinct organisations. (4) ~~This parallelism is supported by another parallel, but directly opposite, class of facts~~; namely, that (5) the vigour and fertility of all organic beings are increased by slight changes in their conditions of life, and that (6) the offspring of slightly modified forms or varieties acquire from being crossed increased vigour and fertility. So that, on the one hand, (7) <u>considerable changes in the conditions of life and crosses between greatly modified forms, lessen fertility</u>; and on the other hand, (8) <u>lesser changes in the conditions of life and crosses between less modified forms, increase fertility.</u>

Diagrammed:

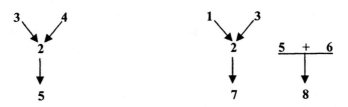

In the first example, the compound argument comprises three simple arguments. Statement two is supported by statements three and four. Statement two, in turn, is given in support of statement five—the ultimate conclusion. The second compound argument is really two arguments, since the conclusion is two separate statements supported by separate chunks of evidence.

MULTIPLE REASONS

Often two or more premises are given for the same conclusion. Here you must decide whether the premises work together to support the conclusion—i.e., they are dependent—or they work separately—i.e., they are independent.

Dependent Reasons

PREMISES ARE CALLED *DEPENDENT* WHEN THEY MUST BE TAKEN TOGETHER IN SUPPORT OF A CONCLUSION.

Example:

The fish Delphina purchased are foul, since all of the fish at Smedley's Market are foul and Delphina purchased her fish there.

Analysis:

(1) <u>The fish Delphina purchased are foul,</u> (since) (2) all of the fish at Smedley's Market are foul and (3) Delphina purchased her fish there.

Diagrammed:

Independent Reasons

PREMISES ARE CALLED *INDEPENDENT* WHEN EACH IS A SEPARATE REASON IN SUPPORT OF A CONCLUSION.

Example:

The fish Delphina purchased are foul, since they had a bad smell when she bought them and she left them out on the counter overnight.

Analysis:

(1) <u>The fish Delphina purchased are foul,</u> (since) (2) they had a bad smell when she bought them and (3) she left them on the counter overnight.

Diagrammed:

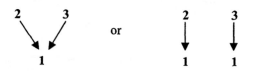

Note here that the diagrammatical representations are the same. Each says that statements two and three independently support statement one. Thus, the links from two to one and three to one must be assessed independently of each other. We shall be using the representation on the left throughout.

DUAL CONCLUSIONS

A premise can support more than one conclusion, yet this is rare.

Example:

Žydrūnas hoisted the massive, 250-kilogram boulder from the earth. So, he'll be exhausted this evening and the frustration of failing to lift it before is over.

Analysis:

(1) Žydrūnas hoisted the massive, 250-kilogram boulder from the earth. (So) (2) he'll be exhausted this evening and (3) his frustration from failing to lift it before is over.

Diagrammed:

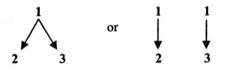

MODULE 13
10 Diagrammatical Tips

As we have seen in Module 12, arguments can be agonizingly complex. Consequently, any attempt to diagram a complex and lengthy argument can be a daunting task. This module offers ten tips, which, through assimilation, will make the task of diagramming much less daunting.

TIP 1
TREAT A CONDITIONAL SENTENCE AS A SINGLE STATEMENT.

A *conditional* sentence functions as a single statement that asserts a special relationship between its antecedent (the "if" part) and consequent (the "then" part): It asserts that the truth of the antecedent is sufficient to guarantee the truth of the consequent—not that its antecedent or its consequent is true. The link between antecedent and consequent is not evidentiary, however, so conditionals are not arguments, though a conditional can be a premise or a conclusion of one. A conditional, then, is a compound statement whose separate parts, because of the function of if-then statements, do *not* make separate statements.

Example:

If *The Village of Stepanchikovo* was written by Dostoyevsky, it could not have been written as satire.

Here neither "*The Village of Stepanchikovo* was written by Dostoyevsky" nor "It could not have been written as satire" are being asserted as true. What is being asserted is that the truth of the antecedent is sufficient to guarantee the truth of the consequent, and without the consequent being true, the antecedent cannot be true. Schematically:

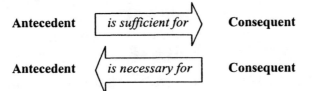

| Antecedent | *is sufficient for* | Consequent |

| Antecedent | *is necessary for* | Consequent |

Some words indicative of conditionals: if, if ... then, when, whenever, is contingent upon, is necessary for, is sufficient for, unless (i.e., if not), only if, provided that, on condition that.

Standard form:

If I don't get a job, then I'll go hungry.

Alternative forms:

Going hungry *is contingent upon* not getting a job.
I'll go hungry *unless* I get a job.
Whenever I don't get a job, I go hungry.
Not getting a job *is sufficient for* going hungry.
Going hungry *is necessary for* not getting a job.
I go hungry, *when* I don't get a job.
I don't get a job *only if* I go hungry.
Provided that I don't get a job, I'll go hungry.
I'll go hungry *on condition that* I don't get a job.

TIP 2
TREAT A SENTENCE WHOSE MAJOR CONNECTIVE IS "OR" AS ONE STATEMENT.

Examples:

Alexander will become president of the Elks Club or he'll quit the Elks.

Donika will grab a soda or she'll go to the beach.

When statements in a sentence are connected by the word "or" as the primary connective, in effect, the whole sentence makes one statement, as it asserts that the whole sentence is true if *at least one* of the disjunctive parts is true.

In the first example, the use of "or" is exclusive in that the disjunctive statement asserts that *only one* of the disjunctive parts is true.

In the second example, "or" is best taken as inclusive in that the statement does not rule out that Donika will both grab a soda and go to the beach.

TIP 3
BREAK UP A SENTENCE WHOSE MAJOR CONNECTIVE IS "AND."

Examples:

Roxanne went to the dance and she drank too much wine.

Roxanne and Alexander went to the dance.

In the first example, "and" functions such that, when it is the primary connective in a sentence, that sentence is true *only when all* of the conjunctive parts are true. In short, each conjunctive part makes a separate statement.

In the second example, there are two statements—"Roxanne went to the dance" and "Alexander went to the dance"—but for convenience in diagramming, there is no need to break up such conjunctive statements.

TIP 4

LEARN TO IDENTIFY THE MAJOR CONNECTIVE OF A LARGE SENTENCE WITH MORE THAN ONE CONNECTIVE.

I give several examples here of sentences with more than one connective. Without being able to identify the major connective, you will not know how many statements each comprises.

1) Whenever Janine finds herself with nothing to do, she gets antsy and she puts on some jazz.

2) Either Courtney will get some tea and Felicia will get a sandwich or Andy will get himself a beer.

3) Both Rodney ran the race in splendid time or Wilma gets angry and Rodney did not run the race in splendid time.

4) Bambi will not sing, unless she is fitfully paid and treated with respect.

5) Embricia will not be angry provided that her exercise machine arrives, and she will do some yoga later.

Analyses:

1) This is a conditional whose consequent, bracketed below, is a conjunction. Treat it as one statement.

Whenever Janine finds herself with nothing to do, [she gets antsy *and* she puts on some jazz].

2) This could be a conjunctive or a disjunctive statement, but the word "either" tells us that it is a disjunction whose first disjunctive part, bracketed, is a conjunction. Treat it as one statement.

Either [Courtney will get some tea *and* Felicia will get a sandwich] *or* Andy will get himself a beer.

3) This could be a disjunction or a conjunction, but the word "both" disambiguates this sentence as a conjunction, comprising two statements.

(1) *Both* [Rodney ran the race in splendid time *or* Wilma gets angry] *and* (2) Rodney did not run the race in splendid time.

4) This could be a conditional or a conjunction. The comma after "sing" and the fact that both simple statements seem to follow from the antecedent show that it is a conditional.

Bambi will *not* sing, *unless* she is fitfully paid *and* treated with respect.

5) The comma here is crucial for disambiguating the sentence. It shows "and" to be the main connective. Without the comma, it would be a lengthy conditional with a conjunctive antecedent.

(1) Embricia will not be angry *provided that* her exercise machine arrives, *and* (2) she will do some yoga later.

In every example, lack of *disambiguators* (key words or punctuation marks) would make it impossible to decide what the major connective of the sentence is. For instance, without "either" in example two or "both" in example three, the sentence literally is ambiguous (i.e., it is impossible to tell whether two is a conjunction or a disjunction and whether three is a disjunction or a conjunction).

TIP 5
BE CAUTIOUS OF WORDS WITH CONCESSIVE FORCE.

In sentences with concessive words—"but," "yet," "although," "nevertheless," "though," "on the contrary," etc.—what is being conceded, in many cases, is irrelevant to the argument and should be left out.
Example₁:

> [Although] (1) you want to be at the convention, (2) you will not, (for) (3) you do not have the money for travel and (4) you will not be able to take time off from work to attend.

Statement one, "you want to be at the convention," which follows the concessive word "although" (boxed), is irrelevant to establishing "you will not [be at the convention]" as true. Simply omit it from consideration.
Diagrammed:

Example₂:

(1) Now to ask whether it is reasonable to believe in scientific conclusions comes right down to asking whether one ought to fashion his beliefs on the basis of the available evidence. But (2) this is what it means to be rational. (Hence) (3) the question amounts to asking whether it is rational to be rational. (Wesley Salmon, "An Encounter with David Hume")

Here the concessive statement, statement two, *is* relevant to the argument, because we cannot justify the conclusion without statements one and two. That is why I advocate the mere exercise of caution.

Diagrammed:

Example₃:

(1) Moderation in the affections and passions, self-control, and calm deliberation are not only good in many respects, but (2) even seem to constitute part of the intrinsic worth of the person; but (3) they are far from deserving to be called good without qualification, although (4) they have been so unconditionally praised by the ancients. For (5) without the principles of a good will, they may become extremely bad, and (6) the coolness of a villain not only makes him far more dangerous, but (7) also directly makes him more abominable in our eyes than he would have been without it. (Immanuel Kant, *Grounding for the Metaphysics of Morals*)

Diagrammed:

In this dense bit of text, there are four separate concessive words, each boxed. The second "but" functions to eliminate everything before it as part of the argument. What follows is the conclusion—statement three. What follows "although" is also irrelevant. The final concessive statement, statement seven, is relevant to the conclusion.

TIP 6
TAKE THE WORD "AND" GENERALLY TO INDICATE THAT EACH OF THE CONJUNCTIVE STATEMENTS THAT ARE LINKED COME TO PLAY AT THE SAME LEVEL IN THE DIAGRAM.

Example:

(1) Older people and sour people do not appear to be prone to friendship. For (2) there is little pleasure to be found in them and (3) no one can spend his days with what is painful or not pleasant, since (4) nature appears to

avoid above all what is painful and to aim at what is pleasant. (Aristotle, *Nicomachean Ethics*)

In the argument above, the word "and" is not a reasoning indicator. It tells us only that statements two and three function at the same level in the diagram. The word "for" indicates that two and three are premises for statement one. Following this tip, then, we can take statements two and three either as dependent reasons for the conclusion or as independent reasons for the conclusion. Here, they are dependent reasons, for statement three supplements what statement two asserts. Thus, Tip 6 is not meant to be an infallible rule, but a general guideline.

Diagrammed:

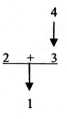

TIP 7
KEEP EXAMPLES OUT OF THE ARGUMENT.

Examples, when correctly used by writers, function to illustrate a certain point, without justifying that point.

Example:

> (1) Remember that no matter what nature may have produced or may be producing, the means must necessarily have been adequate, must have been *fitted to that production.* (2) <u>The argument from fitness to design would</u> <u>consequently always apply, whatever were the product's character.</u> (3) The recent Mont-Pelée eruption, for example, required all previous history to produce that exact combination of ruined houses, human and animal corpses, sunken ships, volcanic ashes, etc., in just that one hideous configuration of positions. (William James, *Pragmatism—A New Name for Some Old Ways of Thinking*)

The third statement functions merely as an illustration of the point being made, not a justification of it. Omit it from consideration.

Diagrammed:

1
↓
2

Yet examples can sometimes be used in a justificatory sense. Consider:

1) Collies are the friendliest dogs, as my collie is very friendly.

2) Collies are the friendliest dogs. My collie, for instance, is very friendly.

3) Collies are the friendliest dogs, as my collie, for instance, is very friendly.

Of these, the first is manifestly justificatory, though one instance makes for an appallingly bad inductive argument. The second should not be taken as an argument, as the second sentence merely illustrates the first. The third is best taken as an argument, given the word "since." However, there seems to be a confusion of aims with the addition of "for instance," as if the author wishes to offer evidence for "Collies are the friendliest dogs" and give an illustration of it at the same time. Good writers, however, will not use examples as justifications.

TIP 8
IF TWO STATEMENTS SAY THE SAME THING, LEAVE ONE OF THEM OUT OF THE DIAGRAM.

Example:

(1) Coherence alone is not enough for justification because (2) a coherent set of propositions may not be grounded in reality. (3) A fairy tale may be coherent, but that doesn't justify our believing it. Since (4) justification is supposed to be a reliable guide to the truth, and since (5) truth is grounded in reality, (6) there must be more to justification than mere coherence (Schick and Vaughn, *How to Think about Weird Things*).

Here statement two justifies statement one and statement three functions merely as an illustration of statement two. Leave out statement three. Statements four and five justify statement six. However, statements one and six say precisely the same thing, so you can leave one of them out—say, statement one. Now, we are left with statements three, four, five, and six. If statement two justifies statement one and statements one and six are equivalent, then use statement two to justify statement six. But statement two can be left out if it says nothing more than what statements four and five say. It does not however, but it provides additional important information. We are left with statements two, four, and five justifying statement six dependently. They are dependent, because four links justification to truth, five links truth to reality, and two links reality to coherence.

(1) ~~Coherence alone is not enough for justification~~ because (2) a coherent set of propositions may not be grounded in reality. (3) ~~A fairy tale may be coherent, but that doesn't justify our believing it.~~ Since (4) justification is supposed to be a reliable guide to the truth, and since (5) truth is grounded in reality, (6) there must be more to justification than mere coherence.

Diagrammed:

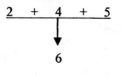

TIP 9
DO NOT BREAK APART A SENTENCE WITH THE WORD "THAT" IN IT, WHEN "THAT" FUNCTIONS CONJUNCTIVELY TO INTRODUCE A DEPENDENT CLAUSE.

Example:

I have often thought that the search for truth is never-ending.

You may be tempted to break this into two statements, "I have often thought" and "the search for truth is never-ending," but here the word "that" tells you that the latter part of the sentence completes the former part. Thus, there is only one statement being made here, so the sentence must be taken as a whole.

TIP 10
WORDS SUCH AS "IN ADDITION," "MOREOVER," "ALSO," "WHAT IS MORE," "BESIDES," "LIKEWISE," "ADDITIONALLY," AND "FURTHERMORE" ARE OFTEN INDICATIVE OF AN ADDITIONAL, INDEPENDENT ARGUMENT.

Example:

(1) God's mercy had been kinder to me than to him [i.e., Origin], (for)(2) it was judged that he had acted most rashly and had exposed himself to no slight censure, whereas (3) the thing had been done to me through the crime of another, thus preparing me for a task similar to his own. Moreover, (4) it had been accomplished with much less pain, being so quick and sudden, (for)(5) I was heavy with sleep when they laid hands on me, and (6) felt scarcely any pain at all (Peter Abelard, *The Secret of my Misfortune*)

Here "moreover" functions to pick out a second, independent line of argument for the conclusion. Diagrammed:

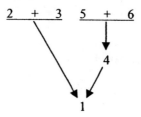

PART IV
WRITING PHILOSOPHY

SECTION A
Preliminaries for Philosophical Essays

MODULE 14
13 General Tips for Writing

TIP 1
BE STRUCTURED

Structure your essays by preparing, in advance, an outline (Module 17) with a thesis included (Module 18). Develop a very narrow thesis for short papers. Tackle a small issue. If the question given to you admits of a lengthy response, narrow your thesis with your teacher's permission to address only some part of the question. You may even want to explain to readers in your introductory section what it is you are not going to try to accomplish in your essay. Overall, never give to readers the sense that there is much more to the issue that is left unsaid by the end of your paper. Let your thesis and outline guide you completely throughout.

TIP 2
BE COHERENT

Coherence of thought demonstrates just how well you understand the issues involved. Present your arguments tightly. Make sure that your paper flows throughout in a manner that makes the overall argument clear to readers. Draw from the readings plentifully, without excessive use of direct quotes, to support the points that you are making, and reference all such points. Excessive use of quotes makes the reading choppy and cut-and-paste. Often it makes the points you wish to make difficult to grasp.

TIP 3
BE RELEVANT

Make sure that everything you write is directly relevant to the issue you are addressing. If you are given a question to answer, answer it directly. Never stray from the topic to shed light on some irrelevant issue in an effort to impress your instructor with your vast knowledge of other issues. Instructors are more impressed by your essay's focus and tightness—at least, they should be—not by your knowledge on irrelevant issues. Remember, there will be other days to write on other issues, if they have such a grip on you. Save irrelevancies for those days.

TIP 4
BE ANALYTICAL

Spend the lion's share of your time developing your thesis with arguments instead of summarizing the readings. Remember that a philosophical essay is a critical analysis of the materials you have been reading and not a summary of them. Break down the arguments you encounter and give a critical assessment of them. It is your own thinking that counts here.

TIP 5
BE FLUID

Write simply and plainly, and avoid verbiage. Strive for fluidity, but not in a stream-of-consciousness manner. Your essays should read easily from sentence to sentence, from paragraph to paragraph. Avoid the use of big words when a simpler word gets across the same point identically. While striving for fluidity, keep in mind the significance of coherence and relevance.

TIP 6
BE CREATIVE

Present your view by trying to find some position on an issue that has not yet been defended, which philosophers sometimes call "finding your own conceptual space." Finding your own conceptual space requires that you first have a good grasp of what others have said on the issue you are addressing. If you defend a thesis similar to someone else's thesis, show clearly how your thesis differs from, and is preferable to, the other thesis. Again, do not spend too much time reviewing in book-report fashion what you are going to evaluate.

TIP 7
BE SYMPATHETIC

Construct digestible paragraphs for your audience. Do not have paragraphs that are so long or dense that readers do not have a chance to catch their breath, so to speak. Remember, the end of each paragraph gives readers a chance to pause and reflect on what was just written. If a paragraph is too lengthy or contains too much information, you can easily lose a reader. Keep paragraphs relatively short and digestible.

TIP 8
BE HONEST

Reference all points you make that need referencing. As a general rule of thumb, if you make any statement and that statement did not originate from you, but came from a reading, then that statement must be referenced. In other words, it is not just direct quotes that require referencing. Failure to do so amounts to stealing ideas from another author and that is plagiarism. Plagiarism is a very serious offense in academic circles.

TIP 9
BE AUTHENTIC

Stay away from excessive quoting from other sources. That gives a paper a cut-and-paste feel to it. It reads choppily and lacks fluidity. Only quote when (1) the author's wording defies restatement—i.e., it is so perfectly stated that to do other than quote it would be a disservice, but this is very rare—or (2) you are planning on addressing directly something the author has said and there is something about the wording that is crucial to what you are addressing.

TIP 10
BE ACCURATE

If you are evaluating an argument, reconstruct the author's views faithfully and accurately before you begin critical analysis of those views. Sometimes perceived problems with another's view vanish when you take the time to reconstruct accurately the arguments on behalf of it. Here especially the analytic tips and rules for diagramming in Modules 12 and 13 come into play. Remember also the straw-man fallacy.

TIP 11
BE CHARITABLE

If you are not quite sure what an author means by some statement and, for instance, it seems clear that there can be only two possible interpretations, if you must choose between them, then choose the most favorable of the two alternatives. In other words, choose the interpretation that makes best sense of the author's general line of argument. If an author's view is genuinely ambiguous—i.e., if there is more than one possible interpretation that is consistent with the main line of argument and there is no reason to favor one over another—point that out in your criticism. In general, however, stay away from criticizing works you do not fully understand.

TIP 12
BE CAREFUL

When you have finished your essay, proofread it carefully. If possible, have a colleague proof it for you. When proofing, subject the whole essay to critical analysis. Is your thesis clearly stated? Are the arguments on behalf of it plainly presented? Are there grammatical and spelling mistakes? Does your essay deviate from your outline? (See Modules 21 and 22 for more on revising and rewriting your essay.)

TIP 13
BE PROUD

I consider this tip to be the most important tip. The reason is this: If you can take pride in the process of creating a philosophical essay, then the other tips will be easy to follow. Remember, this is your paper and it has your name just beneath its title. As your work, it is an extension of you and, thus, it tells others much about the type of person you are. Treat it as an artist treats a painting before she signs her name to the canvas of the finished product.

MODULE 15
Tips of Avoidance

The previous module listed 13 general tips, in hortatory form, as preliminaries for writing a good philosophical essay. This module lists a number of things to avoid on your way to constructing a good philosophical essay.

AVOID VAGUE OR AMBIGUOUS CLAIMS.

Examples:

Fromm was a psychologist who dealt with many different and equally difficult issues.

I agree with Mill for the most part, but he made a few points which I believe to be false.

It is believed by some scholars that by the year 2010, we will have doubled the world's knowledge, and every five years after that it will double again. Theoretically, by the year 2015, we should be almost four times as smart as we are now.

In the first example, that Fromm wrote on many different issues is obvious and, so, uninteresting. That each of these was equally difficult is certainly false. The overall problem is the vagueness of "difficult." Remember, philosophy is a discipline that strives for clarity through elimination of such vague claims.

In the second example, the phrase "for the most part" is horribly vague. Moreover, do not say that some of the things Mill said are false, state what those claims are.

In the third example, doubling the amount of knowledge does not make each person four times as smart by 2015, and it will not make those born at 2015 and after four times as smart as those born before. In short, the phrase "four times as smart" makes little sense. It is best to say that the total amount of information available to anyone will have quadrupled by the year 2015.

AVOID BRINGING UP ONE TOPIC ONLY TO SAY THAT YOU WILL GET BACK TO IT LATER.

Example:

Sextus Empiricus lived in the second century A.D. Before we get into his life, the idea of Skepticism must be looked into.

Go into Skepticism first in a paragraph or so, if that is your aim, and then introduce Sextus thereafter.

AVOIDING STATING THE OBVIOUS.

Examples:

Based on the definition of genetic fallacy stated above, it seems that Freud does not commit the genetic fallacy when he traced the origin of religion. This can be seen when looking at his writing.

Rawls begins where most great philosophers do, at the beginning.

Along with the many similarities (between Gandhi and Aristotle) there are also many differences.

In the first example, the last sentence is superfluous. Where else would one expect to find evidence of the genetic fallacy, if not in his writing? The second example is too trite to be included in an essay. The third example is also unneeded. Such simple similarity-and-difference claims are always uninteresting. Stay away from them (see Module 18).

AVOID TALKING OF YOUR OWN MISUNDERSTANDING OF A PAPER OR BOOK IN YOUR ESSAY.

Example:

I do not completely understand Garry's arguments for why pornography is degrading and immoral.

Why write about something you do not completely understand? Read it until you do understand it or write about something else.

AVOID EXAGGERATED CLAIMS.

Example:

I disagree with just about everything Russell has ever written.

This claim would not be a problem, if this student had read everything Russell has written, but it is a good bet that that is not the case. The sentence should be eliminated.

AVOID OSTENTATION.

Examples:

In this essay, I collaborate with John Stuart Mill that individuality benefits the whole of society. Of course, for any of this to partake, there must be individuality.

Contemporary society is riddled with negative constituents that manifest themselves in the varied forms of violence, ignorance, racism, and apathy. It has been argued that these problems stem from an inadequate system of societal indoctrination in the school system, and this must hold at least some marginal degree of truth.

In the first example, the author uses the words "collaborate" and "partake" wrongly. Steer clear from words that you do not completely grasp.

In the second example, the sentences are stodgy, stuffy, wordy, and unclear. You can get the same point across more simply. Rewritten:

Society today is riddled with violence, racism, ignorance, and apathy. Some have argued that these problems are in part the result of defects in our educational system. I agree.

AVOID SELF- OR OTHER-DEPRECATION, WHEN WRITING.

Examples:

Of course, this is just my opinion on this subject, and everything I've said has to be taken with a grain of salt.

Plato's theory of forms is quite ridiculous. Aristotle was a much smarter philosopher.

In the first example, the student's self-deprecation functions to undermine her credibility as someone who is knowledgeable on the subject of her essay. Why would anyone want to read an essay, if everything stated therein had to be taken with a grain of salt? Let your claims stand or fall because of the evidence supporting them.

In the second example, this student engages in other-deprecation. Plato's theory is not at all ridiculous, though it may be wrong. State precisely what it is that you find objectionable about Plato's views and go from there. Hasty criticism of one of the world's greatest thinkers is very presumptuous and betrays great ignorance.

AVOID VOICING YOUR OPINIONS, BELIEFS, FEELINGS, ETC. THAT CONCERN THE WRITING OF THE ESSAY.

Examples:

I found Searle's essay to be difficult reading.

So how necessarily does one educate man so that he's wise in the area of conflict? Please excuse the use of the word "man" instead of "mankind." I'd rather address the human race as man as opposed to mankind. This by no means is a chauvinistic move on my part. It's merely a way for me to address the human race in a more personal way.

The first example is a claim that has absolutely nothing to do with the development of a thesis. Leave it completely out. Remember, formal papers are not journal entries.

The second example gives three sentences that take readers nowhere and should have no part in a philosophical essay. This student goes off on a stream-of-consciousness tangent.

AVOID, OR USE SPARINGLY, ITALICS.

Example:

Alexander has a mind uncluttered by *trivial* concerns.

The sense of this sentence is clear enough without having to italicize "trivial." Italicizing the word suggests that readers will not get the sense of the claim without emphasis, which is unlikely. If you insist on using italics, do so sparingly.

AVOID BRINGING UP AN INTERESTING, ISOLATED POINT AND LEAVING IT UNEXPLAINED OR UNJUSTIFIED.

Examples:

I feel it evident that Freud's argument of the origins of religion is, in fact, faulty. It seems that under the right circumstances, Freud could be right in his beliefs....

Diogenes was also referred to as "Socrates gone mad." ...

In the first example, the first statement is never justified in the rest of the paper. The second claim, though vague, seems that it might be informative, if spelled out clearly. The biggest problem is that nothing further is said concerning it. Readers, then, are teased with the expectation that something will be said about the claim later. When nothing is said, readers become frustrated.

The second example is a very engaging claim. Yet this writer says nothing more on the issue. It needs elaboration. Otherwise, it should be omitted.

AVOID INSIPID CLAIMS.

Examples:

Some perverted acts, like necrophilia, are clearly wrong and therefore immoral. It is not right to take advantage of a corpse.

All reasons or examples set aside, I believe that homosexuality is not immoral.

In the first example, a corpse is a dead, non-sentient human being. How can one take advantage of something non-sentient? That, of course, is a sign that this student did not spend much time rereading and revising the essay.

In the second example, why would anyone, writing a paper on philosophy, something that is essentially critical, want to set aside examples and especially reasons?

AVOID WORDY EXPRESSIONS.

Examples:

Instead of ...	Choose ...
There is no doubt that...	Doubtless...
She is a woman who...	She...
His account is a false one.	His account is false.
This is a subject that...	This subject...
...used for pedagogical purposes...	...used for pedagogy...
...the question as to ...	...whether...
...call your attention to the fact that...	...remind you...
...owing to the fact that...	...since...
The author tries to make her point by...	She states...

There are, of course, numerous other instances of verbosity. As a rule, once you have finished a paper, go through it thoroughly and try to simplify, wherever you can.

AVOID SEPARATE FORMS OF EXPRESSION FOR COORDINATE IDEAS.

Example:

> The science of biology is fertile, while the mathematical science is sterile.

There is really nothing horribly wrong with the sentence, but it may be expressed more smoothly, if the coordinate ideas are given the same, instead of a different, expression. Rewritten:

> The science of biology is fertile, while the science of math is sterile.

Here the rewritten form has clarity of exposition and smoothness that the example lacks. It is even, I dare say, a bit more elegant.

AVOID METAPHORICAL EXPRESSIONS.

Examples:

> Even though his ignorance may be apparent, his intelligence stings like a sword as he cuts Gorgias with several blows.

> One topic that I do not think that a lot of people take a step back to evaluate is how individuality plays a part in progressive societies. Many times people just go with the flow of what is happening in their lives, and do not think twice if someone who is higher up on the ladder may have made the wrong decision.

> The series of speeches in *Symposium* are not simply meant as beating around the bush that leads us to the main event.

Metaphors may be fun to put into papers, but there is little use for them in papers on philosophy. Philosophy is about clarity and metaphors detract from clarity. The first example creates a vivid, but tremendously exaggerated scenario that is very misleading. It also contains a mixed metaphor: swords do not sting. Examples two and three are vague.

AVOID INTRODUCING A PASSAGE BY TALKING ABOUT ITS LOCATION IN A PARTICULAR PUBLICATION.

Example:

> In his paragraph beginning on page 127, MacIntyre says....

Put this information in a footnote or in parentheses at the sentence's end.

AVOID ATTRIBUTION OF CONFUSION TO AN AUTHOR.

Example:

> Hume was confused by this issue.... He probably did not make this issue clear for the issue itself cannot be cleared up by Hume.

David Hume was a philosopher noted for exceptional lucidity. A thorough reading and rereading of his work would likely show this student that the confusion was not Hume's.

AVOID USING YOUR OWN PERSONAL EXPERIENCE AS EVIDENCE FOR A GENERALIZATION.

Example:

> From my own experience, I've found competition in sport doesn't have deleterious consequences, so it's hard to believe it can be harmful to society.

This student uses personal experience to show that competition in sport does not have harmful consequences to society. That amounts to sloppy inductive reasoning (see "hasty generalization," Module 10). Look for extensive empirical support for generalizations such as this one. Use your own experience merely as additional confirmation or as an illustration.

AVOID SWEEPING, POORLY SUPPORTED GENERALIZATIONS OR BOLD CLAIMS.

Example:

> I strongly disagree with the article "Is Our Admiration of Sports Heroes Fascistoid?" written by Torbjörn Tännsjö.

One cannot "strongly disagree" with a whole article. That, I suppose, amounts to disagreeing with each and every claim. One can disagree with its thesis, many of its claims, or the general tenor of its line of argument. State precisely what you find objectionable.

AVOID PASSIVE-VOICE CONSTRUCTIONS.

Example:

> Plato's views were thoroughly criticized by Aristotle.

Rewritten:

Aristotle thoroughly criticized Plato's views.

Choose active-voice constructions instead. In general, the active voice gives readers a sense of involvement that is lacking with the passive voice. It is also slightly less wordy.

MODULE 16
Common Mistakes

Misplaced Participial Phrases

Examples:

Beatrice told the truth to Alush, not being one to lie.

Being the person best suited for the job, the president hired Rose immediately.

In the first example, the participial phrase, "not being one to lie" modifies "Alush," since it follows it directly. It should follow directly after "Beatrice," as it seems clear that it is Beatrice that is the one who is not disposed to lying. Correctly stated, "Beatrice, not being one to lie, told the truth to Alush," or "Not being one to lie, Beatrice told the truth to Alush."

In the second example, placing the participial phrase just before "the president" implies that "the president" is being modified, not "Roseanne." Rewritten:

The president immediately hired Rose, being the best person for the job."

Problems with Pronouns

Examples:

Nevea and Phoenicia agreed to split the check, but when the check came, she refused to pay anything.

Each person thinks it is their right to choose freely their own spouse.

Every person should do his duty to society.

In the first, to whom is "she" referring, Nevea or Phoenicia? That needs to be cleared up.

In the second, there is a plural pronoun, "their," when the subject, "each person," is singular. More and more this is becoming acceptable today, though it should not be acceptable. Plural pronouns refer to plural nouns.

The third example uses "his," a masculine pronoun, to complement the subject, "every person," which is not gender-specific. Such usage is often seen to be sexist today. Often people say, "Every person should do his or her duty to society." This is inelegant and wordy, but there are not many happy alternatives. One solution is to choose plural nouns and pronouns: "All people should do their duty to society."

Who and Whom

Some examples will suffice here to help clear up confusion. As a rule, the pronouns "who" and "whom" should follow the noun that they are modifying.

Amy, *who* was a constant participant in rugby matches, played viciously and aimlessly.

Amy, *whom* the crowd loved to boo, finally quit the team.

Alexander fell in love with Roxanne, *who* had earlier snubbed his advances.

Alexander fell in love with Roxanne, *whom* he had earlier detested.

"Renquist gave the ring to *whomever*" (since "whomever" follows a preposition) instead of "Renquist gave the ring to *whoever*."

"Renquist gave the ring to *whoever* wanted it" (since "whoever," though following a preposition, is the subject of the phrase following it).

There you'll find Aristander, *whom* you'll see you can trust to interpret your dream.

Which and That

Choose "which" for restrictive clauses and "that" for non-restrictive clauses. A restrictive clause functions to define a term further—i.e., restrict its meaning. A non-restrictive clause gives additional, non-definitional information about a term.
Example:

The puck, which is an exact replica of the one used during the Stanley Cup finals, was on sale for ten dollars.

The puck that you wanted to buy cost me ten dollars.

The first is a restrictive clause; the second is a non-restrictive clause.

Some Other Suggestions to Avoid Mistakes

Abbreviations: Write out all abbreviations, with the following exceptions: "ca." for *circa*, "e.g." (*exampli gratia*) for "for example," "et al." for *et alii* (and others), "ibid." for *ibidem* (in the same place), "vol." or "vols." for "volume" and its plural.

Colloquialism: Avoid all colloquialisms (street words). "Azriel is attractive" instead of "Azriel is a phat dude."

Comma vs. Colon: Use a comma before a quote containing a single sentence. Use a colon for a quote with several sentences.

Comma vs. Period: Commas and periods should be placed inside of the last of two quotation marks. "Angela is not angry," Pomona said, "she's merely being intellectual."

Conjunctions: In general, avoid beginning a sentence with a conjunction such as "yet," "but," or "and." Conjunctions such as "moreover" and "furthermore" are not problematic.

Months vs. Seasons: Months are capitalized; seasons are not.

Numbers: Spell out only numbers before 10. "The three brothers each ate 11 hotdogs."

"Of" with Apostrophe: "That was a distinction of Nozick's" should read "That was Nozick's distinction" or "That was a distinction of Nozick." "Of" in the first sentence implies possession so the apostrophe and "s" are redundant.

Prepositions: Never end a sentence with a preposition. Use "Evolution is the topic about which I wanted to talk" in preference to "Evolution is the topic I wanted to talk about." In common speaking, though, the latter does not seem so stuffy.

Semicolon vs. Colon: A semicolon (;) separates two complete sentences that are intimately linked; a colon (:) does not. "Marcus gave the speech that won the day; Quintus bowed out willingly." "Marcus gave three speeches: one on friendship, one on love, and one on death."

Sentences: Always use sentences in formal writing. "A common enough belief shared by millions." This is not a sentence, but a modifying clause. Sentences must have minimally both a subject and a verb.

Split Infinitives: Never split an infinitive. "Flanders loves *to read* quickly" instead of "Flanders loves *to* quickly *read*."

"That" and Direct Quotes: Never preface a direct quote with the word "that." "That" should be used when you paraphrase what someone has said, not when you quote from that person. "Shelly says that 'Justice is the most important virtue'" should read either as "Shelly says, 'Justice is the most important virtue'" or as "Shelly says that justice is the most important virtue."

Times: Write "1 a.m.," "3 p.m.," and "1:15 a.m." and "3:33 p.m."

Verb "To Be": "The man with the red suit is me" should read "The man with the red suit is I." The verb "to be" always takes the nominative case. "It is I" and not "It is me."

World Wide Web or Web: Capitalize, when using either.

Word Group as Adjective: When a grouping of words is used together as an adjective, hyphenate this grouping. "Nikon is a dyed-in-the-wool anarchist."

MISUSING WORDS

Accept vs. Except: "Accept" does not mean "except." The former means to take or undertake something willingly, while the latter is generally used as a preposition meaning not including.

Adverse vs. Averse: The former means "unfavorable," the latter means "reluctant."

Afterward: not afterwards.

Allude vs. Elude: "Allude" is a casual reference to something; "elude" means to escape from or to avoid.

Altogether: "Altogether" is one word; not "all together."

Among vs. Between: Choose "between" when referring to two things; otherwise use "among."

And/Or: This is tedious and affects the flow of text. "Khaled or Neh went to buy milk, or both," not "Khaled and/or Neh went to buy the milk."

Annual: Only for events that have run three consecutive years.

As vs. Like: "As" is used before phrases and clauses ("Petronia ate all her food, as is proper for a little girl"); "like" functions before nouns and pronouns ("Petronia eats meats like pork, chicken, and beef").

Basically, etc.: Avoid the use of qualifiers, such as "rather," "very," "little," "basically," and "somewhat." E.g., "That was a pretty good effort."

Biannual vs. Biennial: "Biannual" is every six months; "biennial" is every two years.

Can vs. May: "Can" refers to ability or potentiality; "may" relates to permission.

Can Possibly...: "Tanya can possibly..." is redundant. Simply write "Tania can..." or "It is possible for Tanya...."

Can not: This is one word: "cannot."

Capital vs. Capitol: "Capital" is a city; "capitol" is a building.

Comprise: "Comprise" does not mean compose. Use it to mean "is composed of." E.g.: "Animals comprise a circulatory system and a respiratory system."

Continual vs. Continuous: "Continual" is a steady, repetitious cycle; "continuous" means without pause.

Criterion vs. Criteria: "Criterion" is the singular of this noun; "criteria" is its plural. The same goes for "phenomenon" and "phenomena," "curriculum" and "curricula," "datum" and "data."

Currently vs. Presently: "Currently" means up to and including this instant; "presently" means from this instant onward.

Decimate: does not mean to destroy, but literally to reduce by one-tenth.

Declares, etc.: Do not use "declares," "promulgates," or "proclaims," when quoting another author. Use instead "says" or "states."

Despite vs. In Spite of: The former means notwithstanding; the latter adds the sense of defiance.

Destroy Totally/Annihilate Totally: To destroy/annihilate something totally is redundant.

Different from vs. Different than: Choose "different from" instead of "different than."

Discreet vs. Discrete: The former means wise, chary, or circumspect; the latter means separate events or items.

Disinterested: "Disinterested" does not mean "uninterested." The latter means "having no interest," while the former means "having no passion," which is consistent with having interest.

E-mail: Use a hyphen.

Eminent, Imminent, and Immanent: meaning famous, impending, and a belief or suspicion unique to oneself.

Enamored: Used "enamored of," not "enamored with."

Ensure vs. Insure: to make sure as opposed to guard against possible ill effects.

Entitled vs. Titled: Books are "titled," not "entitled." Someone who has inherited or earned some right is "entitled."

Etc.: Avoid, at all costs, the use of "etc." in formal essay-writing. Either give a complete listing of items or narrow your list by saying something like "Philosophers—*such as* Plato, Aristotle, and Epicurus—valued justice highly."

Farther vs. Further: "Further" relates to time or quantity; "farther" relates to distance.

Flounder vs. Founder: "Flounder" is to flop around; "founder" is to run aground and break apart (generally used of ships).

Forgo vs. Forego: to do without vs. to go before.

Former: The pitcher is a former Cy-Young winner and not "The pitcher was a former Cy-Young winner." Choose the latter only if the person is deceased.

Hopefully: An adverb meant to go along with a verb. Not "Hopefully, I can lose 10 pounds."

If, ... than: "If you like coffee, *then* you'll like this blend." Conditionals are designated by "if..., then..." and not "if..., than." "Than" is used for comparisons. "Five is greater *than* four."

Interesting: Stay away in most cases from the word "interesting." "Jung's theory of dreams is interesting." That follows from the fact you are writing about it. Also, it begs the question: In what ways is it interesting? State what is interesting about it at first.

Irregardless: "Irregardless" is not a word. Use "regardless" or "irrespective."

Iterate vs. Reiterate: "Iterate" means to repeat, so to reiterate is to repeat again. The latter is generally used, when the former is meant to be used.

It's: "It's," used possessively, is "its." As a rule remember that "it's" has only one meaning: "it is."

Junior/Senior: Use "Jr." and "Sr." and do not include commas. "Ralph Pistachio Jr."

Lay vs. Lie: Do not confuse "lay" with "lie." "Lay" means to put or set down and it requires a direct object, while "lie" means to assume a horizontal position. It is "lay, laid, laid" and "lie, lay, lain."

Literal/Literally: "Literal" and "literally" are sometimes used wrongly for exaggeration. E.g., "Roxanne literally made him cry" does not add anything to "Roxanne made him cry."

Lightning vs. Lightening: "Lightning" is electrical discharge; "lightening" means reducing the weight of a load.

Lots of: Avoid "lots of"; use "much."

Neither ... Nor: "Neither" must be used with "nor," not "or." "Neither" can be used without "nor," when used as the subject of a sentence. "Nor" should not be used without "neither."

Online: "Online" is one word.

Orientate: This is not a word. "Orientation" is and so too is "oriented."

Past Experience: This is redundant. Talk merely of your experience.

Pedal vs. Peddle: "Pedal" is the noun or verb related to bicycles; "peddle" means to sell.

Percent: Write this out. Do not use "%."

Pleonasm: A pleonasm refers to words or phrases that are redundant or in which one implies the other: "Dead corpse."

Podium: One stands on a podium, not behind it.

Pretty: The word "pretty" does more to confuse than clarify meaning.

Preventive: Use in preference to "preventative."

Pupil vs. Student: Use "pupil" for those in eighth grade or below; otherwise use "student."

Rebut vs. Refute: "Rebut" means to argue against; "refute" means to disprove.

Reoccur: Use "recur," "reoccur" is not a word.

Their, There, and They're: "Their" means of or belonging to them, "there" is a noun or adverb indicating place, and "they're" means they are.

Thing: In general, avoid the word "thing." It's too imprecise.

Tortuous/Torturous: Roads are "tortuous" (i.e., twisty); prison cells and classes on critical reasoning are "torturous."

Try And: Use "try to" instead.

Unique: "Beersham is the most unique athlete." "Unique" does not admit of degrees. Instead, "Beersham is a unique athlete."

MISUSING WORDS WITH A PHILOSOPHICAL SENSE

Ambiguity vs. Vagueness: "Ambiguity" occurs when a word has more than one meaning; "vagueness" occurs when the meaning of a word is unclear.

A Priori vs. A Posteriori: The first means prior to (i.e., independent of) sense experience; the second means after (i.e., coming from) sense experience.

Contradict: There is no need to modify the verb "to contradict." It is superfluous to say "This completely contradicts that." Contradictions do not admit of degrees.

Demonstrate, Prove: Avoid the words "prove" and "demonstrate" for non-deductive arguments. They make for very strong claims. Instead of, "In this paper, I prove…" choose "In this paper, I argue…." Instead of, "Since Corbin hasn't shown much the last three times, this demonstrates that he won't show much this time" choose "Since Corbin hasn't shown much the last three times, it is probable he won't show much this time."

Enormity vs. Enormousness: "Enormity" has to do with morally condemnable actions. When referring to something's awesome size, choose "enormousness." The former is essentially a philosophical term; the latter is not.

Epicurean: Used today adjectivally to designate refinement of taste concerning food and wine, though the philosopher Epicurus, advocating a life of pleasure through avoidance of pain, shunned such extravagance and ate and drank simply.

Ethics: Use with a singular verb.

Infer vs. Imply: "Infer" does not mean "imply." Use "imply" for sentences or statements. "'All philosophers are lovers of wisdom' implies that Aristotle is a lover of wisdom." Use "infer" for mental activity. "Holmes inferred from the size of the hat that the owner was highly intellectual."

Logical: Stay away from the word "logical." To say of something that it is logical is to say that there is no contradiction involved in its use, which is, in effect, to say not much at all. Choose instead something like "reasonable" or "sensible."

Necessary Condition: To say that a condition is necessary does not allow for one to speak of its degree of necessity. Necessity does not admit of degrees. "Habit is more necessary than choosing in determining the moral correctness of an action" is wrong.

Philosophy: The word "philosophy," properly used, does not have a plural sense. It refers to the discipline in which philosophers are engaged. It makes no more sense to say "their philosophies…" than it does to say "their biologies…" or "their psychologies…." So, instead of "the philosophies of the two men…" choose something like "the ideas of the two men…" or "the views of the two men…."

Skeptic: Used and used rightly to indicate one who suspends judgment on philosophical issues, but it indicates that the person suspending judgment is seeking, not indifferent to, a solution.

True: Never speak of degrees of truth. Thus, avoid claims such as "There is some truth to that statement." Write instead something like "The statement should be considered further."

Validity: In general, stay away from the word "validity," when writing. It has a technical sense in deductive reasoning and is out of place in other uses—especially in papers on philosophy. Validity is used to assess deductive arguments, not statements. It is wrong to say "The statement has no validity"; say instead, "The statement is false."

SECTION B
Writing Philosophical Essays

MODULE 17
Preparing an Outline

WHY WRITE AN OUTLINE?

When writing a critical essay, one of easiest mistakes to make is straying from the assigned question. Straying is a mistake of irrelevance. That does not always seem so bad, for writers often stray in ways that are, at least, attention-grabbing or intellectually stimulating. The problem is this: You have promised readers one thing, but have delivered another. Imagine ordering a large vegetarian pizza from the shop on the corner and having a small meat-lover's pizza delivered to your door. You would not at all be satisfied if the delivery person should reply gruffly, "You asked for a pie and I brought you a pie!"

The best way to prevent straying from the assigned question is to prepare in advance an outline for your essay—a sketch of your plan for tackling the assigned question. An outline gives your essay *focus* and focus is crucial for writing a forceful critical essay.

An outline also gives your paper *balance*. Giving your paper balance is a matter of making sure that all issues you wish to cover are treated fully—i.e., that you do not go into such detail on one issue or argument that another is given short-shrift because of the length requirements of the paper. When you construct an outline well, you should be able to see the balance your paper will have.

An outline also gives you *measurement*. It enables you to structure an essay in advance to meet the length requirements of the paper. Relatively short essays of two to six pages do not allow for much elaboration through many arguments on a philosophical problem, so they need to be focused and to-the-point. Longer essays allow for greater elaboration and more content. A good outline will help you meet the constraints of the assigned length.

The function of an outline is to give you a bird's-eye view of your essay, so keep it short. One-third or one-half page is sufficient for a simple critical essay. Three-quarters or one page is sufficient for a synthetic critical essay. In effect, you do not construct an outline to please your teacher, but to help you write.

CONSTRUCTING AN OUTLINE

One of the best ways of demonstrating how to write a good outline is to say some things about what constitutes a bad outline.

On the one extreme is the outline that is put together after the essay is written so that it mirrors the points of the essay. Such outlines are characteristically lengthy, for some students take each sentence of the essay and put it, in condensed form, into the outline. Students here throw together an outline not to help them with their essay's focus, balance, and length, but to meet the requirements of the class. Such an outline is a complete waste of time.

On the other extreme is the outline that is constructed prior to or after the essay that makes no effort to touch base with the essay. Thrown together in 15 seconds, it looks something like this:

I. Introduction
II. Point One
III. Point Two
IV. Conclusion

Again, students that throw together this "outline" are not concerned with their essay's focus, balance, and length. Such an outline is some indication that the essay was put together with the same effort.

When you seriously construct an outline, there are still several problems to avoid. I list three: overdevelopment, congestion, and underdevelopment. Over-development occurs when your outline goes beyond a summary of the main points of the essay. Here excessive length makes it hard for you to use your outline as a guide for your essay. Congestion occurs when your outline, though not overly lengthy, is overly dense, because you have written out each of the main points in unneeded detail. Here density makes it hard for you to use your outline as a general guide to writing. Finally, underdevelopment occurs when each of the main points of the essay is not represented in the outline. Here missing points makes your outline a faulty guide for writing.

Prepare your outline prior to writing your paper and follow the general schemata, given below, for simple critical essays and synthetic critical essays. As you write your essay, you will often, if not always, find that you must revise your outline. Once you dig into the philosophical material at some depth, you might discover, say, that your thesis is no longer tenable and needs slight revising, perhaps even overhauling, or that your reconstruction of an author's view is mistaken. It is no crime to rework your outline. Expect to do so.

GENERAL FORM OF A SIMPLE CRITICAL ESSAY

General Schema

What follows is a general schema for a simple critical essay—a critical response to a philosophical problem by analysis of a philosophical essay or a part of it. Shoot for no more than three arguments, due to the shortness of the paper.

I. Introduction
    A. Statement of the Problem, say x
    B. Your Thesis
II. Philosopher P's View of x
III. Why P's View Is Wrong*

A. Argument One vs. P

B. Argument Two vs. P

C. Argument Three vs. P

IV. Conclusion

V. Bibliography

Sample Outline for Simple Critical Essay

Assigned Question: What is friendship for Aristotle? Are friendships based on pleasure and utility true friendships for him like those based on virtue?

I. Introduction

    A. Problem: Are friendships based on pleasure and utility real friendships for Aristotle?

    B. Thesis: I argue that of Aristotle's three forms of friendship—pleasure, utility, and virtue—only friendships based on virtue are true friendships.

II. Aristotle's View of Friendship

    A. Friendship Based on Pleasure

    B. Friendship Based on Utility

    C. Friendship Based on Virtue

III. Why Friendships Based on Pleasure and Utility are not True Friendships

    A. Transitory Nature of Pleasure and Utility; Stability of Virtue

    B. True Friendships can be only among Equals; Friendships of Pleasure and Utility are not Friendships among Equals

IV. Conclusion

    A. Summary of Problem

    B. Summary of Solution

V. Bibliography

GENERAL FORM OF SYNTHETIC CRITICAL ESSAY

General Schema

Here is a general schema for a synthetic critical essay—a critical analysis of, and new take on, a philosophical problem by a thorough look at the literature on it.

I. Introduction

    A. Statement of the Problem, say x

    B. Your Thesis

II. Other Philosophers' Views of x.

    A. P's View of x.

    B. Q's View of x.

    C. R's View of x.

III. Problems with Other Philosophers' Views

    A. Arguments vs. P.

    B. Arguments vs. Q.

C. Arguments vs. R.
IV. My Solution
    A. My View of *x*
    B. Why My View of *x* Is Preferable
V. Conclusion

Sample Outline for Synthetic Critical Essay

Assigned Question: Are dreams meaningful phenomena or do we create meaning from random images that flit through our brains, when sleeping?

I. Introduction
    A. Problem: Do dreams have a meaning?
    B. Thesis: Dreams are both psychologically meaningful and physiologically rooted.
II. Traditional Accounts of Dreams
    A. Dreams and the Paranormal
    B. Purely Physiological Account of Dreams
    C. Purely Psychological Account of Dreams
III. Problems with Traditional Accounts
    A. Arguments vs. Dreams and the Paranormal
    B. Arguments vs. Purely Physiological Accounts of Dreams
    C. Arguments vs. Purely Psychological Accounts of Dreams
IV. Dreams are Psychologically Relevant and Have Physiological Dimension
    A. Psycho-Physiological Model of Dreams
    B. Rules out Paranormal
        1. Vs. Prophecy
        2. Vs. Clairvoyance
        3. Vs. Dream Telepathy
    C. Accommodates Recent Psychological Research
        1. Traumatic Dreams
        2. Lucid Dreaming
        3. Recurring Dreams
        4. Affects of Environment/Social Setting on Content
    D. Accommodates Rich Body of Physiological Research
        1. REM and REM-Deprivation
        2. Prodromal Dreams
        3. Bodily States and Dream Content
        4. Pathology and Dream Content
        5. Dreaming and the Brain
V. Conclusion

Keep your outline close at hand when writing. Tape it to the wall or pin it to a board near your computer so that you can use it to keep your essay focused, balanced, and measured. Moreover, it needs to be handy since it is very likely that you will "tweak" your outline along the way. Use it as a guideline.

MODULE 18
Writing a Philosophical Thesis

Your thesis anchors your critical essay by offering a direct answer to the assigned question. It is the conclusion of the main argument of your essay and the remainder of the paper is an attempt to provide arguments on its behalf.

This module offers eight rules to follow to help you construct a good thesis.

RULE 1
GIVE YOUR THESIS A CONTEXT.

Example:

What would you do? I agree with the view that Glaucon expresses and explains. Justice by his definition is self-fulfillment without punishment.

These three sentences were thrown out at the start of a short essay and left on their own—presumably as a thesis. This is a paper that concerns the Glaucon's story of the ring of Gyges from Book II of Plato's *Republic*. Readers unfamiliar with Plato will not know that. Thus, it is essential to give readers a context.

Rewritten:

In Book II of Plato's *Republic*, with his illustration of the ring of Gyges, Glaucon argues that justice is about self-fulfillment without punishment. In this paper, I argue that this view of justice is essentially correct.

RULE 2
AVOID WRITING A VAGUE OR AMBIGUOUS THESIS.

Examples:

The topic I chose to write about is heroes.

In this essay you will read about Socrates' argument with Meletus. This essay has my view of what I thought Socrates meant and it will also critically analyze his argument. I feel that Socrates has an argument that lacks some reasonable thought, and will discuss it in depth. But what if things didn't go the way they did? I will try to explain what might have happened if things were different.

The first thesis tells us something about the general topic of the paper, but nothing about the direction of the paper. What is it about this thesis that would make anyone want to read on?

The last example is nothing more than an attempt at a thesis. Which argument is being referred to? What direction will the analysis take? How does it lack reasonable thought? What are the events referred to and how might they have gone otherwise? Nothing here hooks the reader. Every sentence is vague.

RULE 3
KEEP THE THESIS AND OTHER INTRODUCTORY-PARAGRAPH CLAIMS SIMPLE.

Example:

> In his article "Is Homosexuality Bad Sexuality Because It Is Biologically Unnatural?" Michael Ruse addresses questions regarding the morality, or immorality, of homosexuality. The aim of this paper is to summarize Ruse's claims regarding the morality of homosexuality, citing potential weaknesses that, if corrected, could strengthen the argument. In addition to the summary, a brief discussion regarding an important omission is included. A discussion regarding the perverseness of homosexuality is not included in this paper.

This paragraph does give the reader insight and direction into the paper, but it could and should be simplified.

Rewritten:

> In his article "Is Homosexuality Bad Sexuality Because It Is Biologically Unnatural?" Michael Ruse addresses questions regarding the morality of homosexuality. The aim of this paper is to summarize Ruse's claims and cite potential weaknesses that, if corrected, could strengthen the argument. In addition, I include a brief discussion regarding an important omission.

Here the rewrite is simpler, but still suffers from another problem, which leads us to rule 4.

RULE 4
MAKE YOUR THESIS SPECIFIC.

Example:

> In the essay I am about to write, I would like to discuss the Epicurean view of friendship. Although many have criticized and labeled this view as inconsistent and contradictory, and that is what I would like to discuss.

The second sentence, the thesis, does not say much at all. State precisely what you are going to discuss, but first, set up the problem with something illustrative of Epicurus' view of friendship.

Rewritten:

> Among the fragments that survive, Epicurus gives a view of friendship that is seemingly contradictory. As an egoistic hedonist, he is committed to the view that all things are valuable only insofar as they bring about pleasure, yet he states that friendship, like pleasure, is intrinsically valuable. In this paper, I aim to show that this tension can be resolved.

RULE 5
GO BEYOND DESCRIPTION IN YOUR THESIS; FOCUS ON A CRITICAL ANALYSIS.

Example:

> In John Stuart Mill's book, *On Liberty*, Mill's thesis is written on the opinion that Mill believes the way to deal with an individual who harms others while exercising his idea of liberty is that you must punish them, physically or morally, and teach them right from wrong.

This is a wordy thesis statement that lacks a critical component.

Rewritten:

> In *On Liberty*, Mill argues that those who harm others must be punished or educated. I argue that Mill's thesis is correct, but I shall show that his notion of punishment is too vague to be serviceable.

RULE 6
WRITE A THESIS THAT ENGAGES READERS.

Examples:

> Epicurus' view on justice and friendship is interesting. The views on justice and friendship are well worth comparing, but the interpretation of the Epicurean views on the two are curiously imaginative. In other words, Epicurus had an interesting view on the relationship between justice and friendship.

> The question here is whether Aristotle's doctrine of the mean is a viable ethic for today. My answer and according to what little I understand about Aristotle's ethics is that it is a viable ethic.

In the first example, not only is the thesis vague, it is also uninteresting. Does this make you as a reader want to read on? As I state in Module 16, the word "interesting" should be avoided at all costs in essays. It is vague and can always be replaced by something more specific. What does it mean for the thesis to be "curiously imaginative" and why is that something undesirable?

In the second example, we have an objection similar to that of the prior example. In telling readers that you have a poor grasp of the topic about which you are writing, you not only fail to engage readers, you turn off readers. Imagine a sports analyst who begins a one-hour special on baseball by stating he does not know much about the game he will be critiquing. Would anyone watch?

RULE 7
TRY NOT TO DO TOO MUCH WITH YOUR THESIS.

Example:

> Is winning an obsession for athletes in sports? I will look at aspects of competition with regards to winning. I am also looking into whether the playoff system that has been established in professional sports in the United States actually determines the best team from that season.

Here, in effect, we have two, rather non-specific theses: one on the obsession with winning in sports and another on whether the playoff system determines the best team. Two separate topics make for two papers. Do not force the two into one just because you have something to say about both issues. Choose the topic that most interests you and leave the other aside for another time.

RULE 8
NEVER INTRODUCE YOUR THESIS BY RELATING TO READERS YOUR OWN PERPLEXITY ON THE ISSUE SURROUNDING IT.

Example:

> In reading about scientific realism and scientific anti-realism, I found that both views made very interesting points and found it difficult to decide which argument I prefer. I agreed with the views of each category. After reading about realism and anti-realism again I concluded that I preferred anti-realism more. The type of anti-realism I identify the most with is the paradigm-relativist approach.

Rewritten:

> The debate between scientific realists and anti-realists is intriguing, but I shall argue anti-realists have the more persuasive arguments. Of the various views of anti-realism, I shall argue that the paradigm-relativist approach is the most reasonable.

MODULE 19
Simple Critical Essay

OBJECT OF A SIMPLE CRITICAL ESSAY

The object of a simple critical essay is to develop a thesis that critically addresses, in a short essay, one work—or some part of it, say, one argument—of a particular philosopher. You may be in complete agreement, partial agreement, or complete disagreement with what the author has to say. The point is to argue for your thesis by using evidence and reasons. Also, and this is a point I cannot state too much, try not to do too much with your thesis—especially for short papers. Be modest, but thorough. Being overly ambitious is usually a recipe for disaster.

STEPS FOR WRITING AN EVALUATIVE ESSAY

Step 1: Construct your thesis.

Your thesis tells readers what you will be arguing for. Use that as a guide for the entire essay. While writing, you may find that you wish to narrow it down—i.e., make it more concise and specific—to accommodate the length requirements of your essay and to allow for a thorough analysis of the topic, given the length requirements. However, once you have settled on a thesis that is sufficient for the task you have undertaken, do not stray from it.

Step 2: Embed your thesis into a brief introductory paragraph.

For a very short essay—e.g., one-to-two pages in length—make this introduction very brief. Get to the point quickly. Often two sentences suffice: the first to set up the thesis, the other to present the thesis. Example:

> At *Apology* 25c-26b, Socrates gives the second of three main arguments against his accuser Meletus. *In this paper, I maintain that this argument in itself is enough to show that Meletus is unfit to charge and prosecute Socrates of corrupting the young.*

For longer essays—e.g., three to eight pages—a lengthier introduction is better. That enables you to set up the problem you wish to discuss with utmost clarity. Example:

Apology is a work by Plato that chronicles the life of Socrates through his trial for his life. Being accused of corrupting the young, Socrates stands in defense before two sets of accusers: older and younger accusers. Plato gives an especially vivid account of Socrates' cross-examination of the main representative of the younger accusers—Meletus, who will, as it turns out, be chiefly responsible for the death of Socrates.

While examining Meletus, Socrates gives three arguments that are designed cleverly to show that Meletus is ignorant of just those matters about which he charges Socrates and, thus, that he is unfit to prosecute Socrates. At *Apology* 25c-26b, Plato gives the second of these three—an especially cunning argument aimed to expose Meletus' ignorance. *In this paper, I maintain that this argument in itself is enough to show that Socrates should not have been on trial for the crimes of which he was accused.*

Step 3: Summarize any arguments of the author you will be critiquing.

This should be roughly one-quarter of the paper, no more. Quote directly only if there is something unique about an author's wording that paraphrasing cannot capture. For example, when you wish to show that an author commits the fallacy of ambiguity, you should quote her so that you can show your readers precisely how she commits this fallacy. When summarizing an argument, use the *Principle of Charity*:

ALWAYS RESTATE AN ARGUMENT THAT IS BEING EVALUATED IN ITS STRONGEST POSSIBLE FORMULATION.

Use of the principle of charity greatly reduces any possibility of misrepresenting an argument. Intentional misrepresentation for the sake of easy refutation is called "building up a straw man" (see Module 11).

Step 4: Expose the weakness(es) that author's argument(s) through arguments of your own.

Your critical analysis should be roughly one-half of the paper. What are the points of agreement, if any, between the author's position and your own? Just what do you find objectionable? Examine the best arguments of the author's thesis you are addressing. In doing so, you will be putting forth arguments of your own. Present your arguments with an eye to maximum clarity. That requires simplicity of expression and steering clear of vagueness and ambiguity. Clarity and simplicity enable you to communicate convincingly with the largest possible audience, which is, to all intents and purposes, the aim of philosophy.

Step 5: Reference all material, whether paraphrasing or quoting.

Examples:

In one study of two groups of athletes—those who professed to use amply psychological tactics in athletic performance and those who claimed that they never use such tactics—no statistically significant differences were found in overall performance of both groups (Bunderkrufts 2001, 69).

Freud (1927, 67) said that god the father is a free creation of our wish impulses and has no basis in reality.

The first example refers to a particular study. The author's name, unmentioned in the text, is given in parentheses, along with the year and the page of the published work in which it is to be found. In the second example, since Freud is mentioned in the text, his name need not be placed prior to the year of his work. Readers can find a full reference to the two works in your bibliography.

Step 6: Summarize your argument.

Walk readers through a brief summary of your entire argument at paper's end. This should be limited to one short paragraph for short papers. As a general, though not inviolable, rule, keep the length of your summary consistent with the length of your introduction. The opening paragraph and conclusion should make up (roughly) no more than one-quarter of the paper.
    Example (back to Plato's *Apology*, short-essay example):

In this essay, I have argued that the second argument that Socrates puts forth against Meletus in his defense is the strongest of the three. I hope to have shown that this argument should have been sufficient to exonerate Socrates from the charge of corrupting the young.

Step 7: Include a title.

A title should be informative, but it can also be clever. Never try to be cute at the expense of being informative, and never mislead.
    Example (again, Plato's *Apology*): Was Socrates' Death Sentence Just?

Step 8: Include a bibliography.

There are several ways to do this. I illustrate just one. Consult your instructor for her preference. Whichever way you choose, just be sure to include all the necessary information. I give three below.

Article:

Holowchak, M. Andrew. (2001). "Individual Happiness and Social Respon-sibility." *Fundamentals of Philosophy, Fifth Edition*. David Stewart and H. Gene Blocker (eds.). Upper Saddle River, NJ, 412-20.

Book:

Holowchak, M. Andrew. (2004). *Critical Reasoning & Philosophy: A Concise Guide to Reading, Evaluating, and Writing Philosophical Works*. Lanham, MD: Rowman & Littlefield Publishers, Inc.

Webpage:

Holowchak, M. Andrew. "Sleeping with Mother, Men, Gods, and Beasts: Virtuous Rule and Vicious Dreams in Republic IX." *Plato: The Internet Journal of the International Plato Society*. February 2001. The International Plato   Society.   11   Nov.   2009.   "http://gramata.univ-paris1.fr/Plato/rubrique7.html."

Always write up a publishing company *precisely* as it appears in a publica-tion. If a company appears as "Smyntner & Smythe, Publishers Inc.," then re-write is just as it is—ampersand and all. In addition, for publishers in American cities that are not commonly known, always include the state—i.e., its two-letter abbreviation—after the city. For instance, in the first example, "Upper Saddle River" is followed by "NJ" and, in the second, "Lanham" is followed by "MD," since it is likely that many, if not most, people do not know where Upper Saddle River and Lanham are.

MODULE 20
Synthetic Critical Essay

OBJECT OF A SYNTHETIC CRITICAL ESSAY

A synthetic critical essay is a larger project than a simple critical essay. In a simple critical essay, you do no more than critically evaluate the philosophical position of a single author on a particular issue. For a synthetic critical essay, you must draw from more than one source of the existing philosophical literature on some issue—usually, the literature introduced in the classroom will be sufficient—and develop your own thesis. In other words, in a critical essay, you go beyond mere criticism of others' views and put forth your own view on some philosophical problem. In general, about half of your paper should relate to what you think about an issue. Some of what is covered in Module 19—i.e., referencing and inclusion of title and bibliography—applies here as well and will not be covered.

STEPS FOR WRITING A SYNTHETIC CRITICAL ESSAY

Step 1: Construct your thesis.

Here everything written in Module 19 applies equally well.

Step 2: Embed your thesis into the introductory section of your paper.

A synthetic critical essay—here I have in mind a paper ranging from, say, eight to 25 pages—is much longer than a simple critical essay. Thus, it comprises introductory and concluding sections, not just introductory and concluding paragraphs.

Here the introductory section, comprising perhaps two or three paragraphs, should set out the philosophical problem to be addressed, give a summary statement of the views of authors to whom you will be responding, and finally set up and set out your thesis. It is, in effect, a summary account of your outline.

Remember, you are trying to draw in readers with this introduction. Make it attention-grabbing, not drab. Be clear also how your view differs from that of other philosophers you will be criticizing. I give two examples below for illustration.

Example$_1$:

The topic "happiness" has traditionally been and continues to be the focal point of and most seductive issue in philosophical discussions in ethics. While many, such as Aristotle and Mill, take it to be the end of all human activity, almost all (if not all) philosophers acknowledge that it is a valuable, if not essential, component of a good life.

Happiness proves puzzling, however. Though we all desire it, few of us seem to be able to secure it. The question becomes: Why is something that is so slippery so desirable?

In this essay, I do not wish to solve the puzzle of happiness. I merely give reasons why it exists. *My paper will center on a notion of happiness being a nesting of three different types of integration: personal, political, and cosmic.*

Note that the puzzle of happiness is a sufficiently broad issue—too broad for even a 20-page essay. Therefore, it is appropriate here to tell readers just what cannot be done in this paper.

Example₂ (student's paper, *Philosophy of Sport*):

To begin I would like to pose a few questions to you, the reader. Who lost the NCAA basketball championship five years ago? Who was beat out in the presidential election in 2000? Who was the first team eliminated in the 2009 Stanley Cup Playoffs? You may be wondering why anyone would even be interested in trying to answer any of these questions. I am fairly certain that the majority of readers (at least those who follow sports and observe politics) would be able to answer any of these questions if they were slightly modified. For instance, who was the winner of the NCAA basketball championship five years ago, or who won our presidential election in 2000? By simply changing the subject from the loser to the winner, we suddenly have a better recollection and associate a greater importance to the answer.

In the next paragraph, this student comments on how we lionize winners and forget all others who do not win—even those people and teams who were very close to winners. That speaks to his thesis, which concerns America's unhealthy obsession with winning.

This is a very clever introduction to an intriguing philosophical issue. It seduces you as a reader by challenging your memory and the challenge sets up the thesis. After reading this introduction, I wanted to read further.

Step 3: Summarize the arguments of the authors you will be critiquing.

As with the simple critical essay, this should take up no more than one-quarter of your paper. When drawing from other sources, use the best or most recent views and offer a critical analysis of those views, insofar as they have impacted the development of your thought.

Again, remember to be charitable. Give the best arguments of the authors you have selected and make doubly sure that there is no misrepresentation of their views. Again, if there is something about an author's own presentation of an argument that you want to address (e.g., ambiguous use of a word or vagueness), you may want to present this argument in the author's own words.

Step 4: Expose the weaknesses of their views.

Why is it that those views cannot be maintained philosophically?
Example (in condensed form):

> Freud maintains that happiness is the immediate satisfaction of dammed up erotic impulses. This view, however, is much too narrow. First, it fails to capture anything of current linguistic usage. Moreover, it conflates the pleasure that is attendant upon sexual release with happiness. That reduces happiness to a type of erotic hedonism that leaves no room for the happiness that attends upon intellectual or aesthetic pursuits. For those reasons, Freud's view cannot be maintained.

Step 5: Present your own view and give arguments on its behalf.

Knocking down contrary views is not enough to defend a thesis. You need to motivate your own view in a positive fashion—i.e., to show why your view is philosophically superior to other views. How does it solve problems or address issues that other views cannot?

Step 6: Point out any weaknesses or deficiencies of your own view.

State conceivable objections to your view and show how they can be remedied. If some objections cannot be remedied fully, show how your view, objections notwithstanding, is still preferable to the other theses you have criticized.

Thinking up objections to your own view is one of the most difficult exercises in philosophy. Here, after you have just spent a considerable amount of time criticizing the views of other thinkers and ferreting out your own bit of conceptual space, you are asked, in effect, to think up ways to destroy your own view. This exercise, however, is not foolish. It is merely a safeguard against putting forth an alternative view that is easily dismantled.

Step 7: Summarize your argument.

Again, the summary, at the end of the paper, should roughly be of the same length as the introduction. One paragraph is usually sufficient for a short essay.

SECTION C
Revising & Rewriting Philosophical Essays

MODULE 21
Motivating a Rewrite

WHY REWRITE YOUR ESSAY?

One obvious answer is that there is the possibility of receiving a better grade. The advantages and disadvantages of writing for a better grade are explored in the following section.

Another answer is that philosophical essays test for a different set of writing skills than do other sorts of essays. Philosophical essays are essentially critical and you cannot merely pop out a critical essay on demand without, first, learning how to think critically and, second, without learning how to write critically. Those skills need to be acquired and honed and the best way to acquire and hone those skills is to practice them. Rewrites, thus, are an important tool.

A third answer is that you cannot expect to write a good essay in one draft. That does not happen for professional philosophers and it will not happen for you. Moreover, any paper, however polished, can always be improved. If you are the sort of person who strives for improvement and expects excellence, you should consider rewriting your essays.

A fourth answer, related to the last two, may be given by anticipating an answer to a question "Why do you work out?" that is asked of someone who works out regularly. The answer would be something like "To improve my physical fitness." Likewise, the answer to the question "Why should you rewrite you philosophical essay?" would be something like "To improve my mental fitness."

The reasons listed above, I believe, are pretty good reasons. None of them, however persuasive, should compel you to write, if your instructor is unwilling to allow you to rewrite. Therefore, consult with your instructor before undertaking a rewrite. (You can always undertake a rewrite for your own sake or perhaps because you wish to submit your paper to an undergraduate conference, but nothing replaces the timely feedback of a professional like your instructor.)

WRITING REWRITES INTO A COURSE

This section, as its title indicates, is written more for instructors than for students.

Students adopt one of several attitudes, when it comes to writing an essay—especially a philosophical essay. On the one extreme, some students balk and complain when they find out that their philosophy course requires critical essays. When they write their paper, they tend to put out a minimal effort—to do just enough to get by. Getting such students to consider rethinking and rewriting an essay is generally time wasted. The majority of students can be motivated to revise and rewrite an essay, if they know they stand a good chance of improving their grade. The problem is that such students generally expect a better grade, regardless of the effort they put into their rewrite and the effort is usually minimal. Instructors are often torn: The student took up the challenge to do a rewrite, but the paper handed in is almost the same as the first. Does the student deserve a better grade? On the other extreme, some students seize upon the chance to rewrite an essay for the challenge of improving it philosophically. The opportunity to receive a better grade is welcome, but the opportunity to improve their grasp of a philosophical problem in a revised and rewritten essay is its own reward. What is the problem here? There is no problem other than that such students are few—too few.

The chief difficulty with offering students the opportunity to rewrite their essays is that such rewrites, if undertaken seriously, often come at the expense of their other course work, both in the same class and in other classes, at the time of the rewrites. To avoid that problem, it is best for instructors wishing to encourage students to rewrite papers to put rewrites into their course syllabi. That, of course, can easily be done in classes that are "writing intensive," where there is a cap on student enrollment. It takes a bit more ingenuity and effort on behalf of the instructor in classes that are not.

Since my aims as a teacher are as much to introduce students to the methods of philosophers as well as to the discipline of philosophy in introductory-level courses, I have found it helpful in introductory-level courses to structure each course thematically so that the material at course's end is cumulative. That way, students learn to do philosophy the same way that professional philosophers do it. They begin by learning to write simple critical essays in preparation for a lengthy synthetic essay to be handed in at the end of the term.

MODULE 22
Suggestions for Revising and Rewriting Essays

As with so many other disciplines, success in writing a good philosophical essay is a matter of hard work and a little sweat. Even for professional philosophers, getting published, especially in the best journals, is difficult. Persistence is the key. Success usually comes through rewriting papers by addressing the comments of colleagues or reviewers. A highly polished paper is generally the result of many revisions; seldom does a professional philosopher get things right the first time. It is the same when you write a philosophical essay for class. Do not expect to write a perfect paper in one draft; that will not happen, even if you are among the best students and writers. Ask classmates to read and give a critical response to your paper. You may be frustrated at first to discover that you seem to be making so many mistakes and that there is so much to learn about writing a solid philosophical essay. Keep plugging away and you will see improvement with each effort. Be patient. By term's end, you will be surprised to see just how much you have learned about writing a tight, persuasive philosophical essay.

In what follows, I recommend some helpful suggestions on revising your philosophical essay that have proven effective in my own classes over the years. Develop your own plan if these recommendations prove unhelpful, or consult with your instructor about ideas that she might have for revising and rewriting your essay.

Revision One

Finish a polished draft of your essay, say, a week before its deadline. Let the paper sit for a day or two, while you move on to other projects. After a couple of days, go back to your paper with a renewed and reinvigorated effort. Inspect the outline for tightness and coherence of thought. Examine again your thesis. Look for tightness and cogency in your arguments on behalf of your thesis. Go through the spell-check menu. Look for problems with grammar. Make sure all points that need referencing are referenced. Inspect the bibliography for completeness. Look over your title. Have a friend or colleague perform the same overall inspection. Write down all the problems with your essay on a separate sheet of paper. You or your reader can use a comment sheet like the one given in Appendix B. Rewrite the paper to address the problems.

Revision Two

This revision should be done in the classroom, just a few days prior to the due date. Bring in two drafts of your paper. Under the direction of your teacher, break into circular groups of, say, three. In clockwise fashion, hand a copy of your paper for critical commentary to the person to your left, while your group members follow likewise—i.e., you receive the paper of the person to your right. Use a photocopy of the comment sheet given in Appendix B for your comments on colleagues' papers. When that has been completed, hand the other copy of your paper to the person to your right to get a second set of comments on your paper, while the two others do the same.

When both sets of comments have been completed, collect them, read them thoroughly—not all will be substantive—and set up a written plan for revising your essay in agreement with these comments. Appendix C is a sample sheet for setting up such a plan. Revise your paper accordingly.

APPENDICES

Appendix A
Some Exercises for Diagramming

Here are some practice exercises to sharpen your evaluative skills through diagramming. Use the tips of Module 13 and diagram each of the following examples.

"It is not too much to say that an educational philosophy which professes to be based on the idea of freedom may become as dogmatic as ever was the traditional education which is reacted against. For any theory and set of practices is dogmatic which is not based upon critical examination of its own underlying principles." John Dewey, *Experience and Education*

"It is desirable, in short, that in things which do not primarily concern others, individuality should assert itself. Where not the person's own character but the traditions or customs of other people are the rule of conduct, there is wanting one of the principle ingredients of human happiness and the chief ingredient of individual and social progress." John Stuart Mill, *On Liberty*

"It seems to me that it is an excellent thing for a physician to practice prognosis. For, if he has foreknowledge and declares beforehand at his patients' beside both the present, the past, and the future, filling in the details they have omitted, it will be believed that he has a better understanding of their cases so that they will have the confidence to entrust themselves to him as their doctor. Furthermore, he would carry out treatment most effectively from foreknowledge derived from the present symptoms of what will be the future course of the disease." Hippocratic author of *Prognostics*

"A little reflection will show that civil disobedience is a necessary part of non-cooperation. You assist an administration most effectively by obeying its orders and decrees. An evil administration never deserves such allegiance. Allegiance to it means partaking of evil. A good man will resist an evil system or administration with his whole soul." Mahandas Ghandi

"If there is some deceiver or other who is supremely powerful and supremely sly and who is always deliberately deceiving me, then I still know that I exist. For let him do his best at deception, he will never bring it about that I am nothing so long as I shall think that I am something. Thus, after this and all other arguments have been most carefully weighed, it must finally be established that this pronouncement 'I am, I exist' is necessarily true every time I utter it or conceive it in my mind." Rene Descartes, *Meditations*

"Though in the state of nature he has a right to property, yet the enjoyment of it is very uncertain, and constantly exposed to the invasion of others: for all being kings as much as he, every man his equal, and the greater part no strict observers of equity and justice, the enjoyment of the property he has in this state is very unsafe, very unsecure." John Locke, *Second Treatise on Government*

"I am persuaded that those who quite sincerely attribute their sorrows to their views about the universe are putting the cart before the horse: the truth is that they are unhappy for some reason of which they are unaware, and this unhappiness leads them to dwell upon the less agreeable characteristics of the world in which they live." *Conquest of Happiness*, Bertrand Russell

"To fear death, gentlemen, is no other than to think oneself wise when one is not, to think one knows what one does not know. No one knows whether death may not be the greatest of all blessings for a man, yet men fear it as if they knew that it is the greatest of evils. And surely it is the most blameworthy ignorance to believe that one knows what one does not know." Plato, *Apology*

"So powerful a prohibition (i.e., taboo versus incest or killing) can only be directed against an equally powerful impulse. What no human soul desires stands in no need of prohibition; it is excluded automatically. The very emphasis laid on the commandment 'Thou shalt not kill' makes it certain that we spring from an endless series of generations of murderers, who had the lust for killing in their blood, as, perhaps, we ourselves have today." Sigmund Freud, "Reflections upon War and Death"

"The peace that it [a just war] establishes must be a clear improvement over what exists. Although there are visions of peace and democracy in Iraq, it is quite possible that the aftermath of a military invasion will destabilize the region and prompt terrorists to further jeopardize our security at home. Also, by defying overwhelming world opposition, the United Nations will undermine the United Nations as a viable institution for world peace." Jimmy Carter, "Just War—or a Just War?" *The New York Times*, March 9, 2003

Appendix B
Teacher/Student Comment Sheet

Read the essay you receive twice. First, read it without an eye for criticism. Try to get a general grasp of the thesis, the main line of argument, and the overall coherence of the essay. Read it a second time and prepare a critical commentary guided by the categories below.

Comments on the Thesis:

Comments on Arguments on Behalf of Thesis:

Comments on Use of Text(s):

Comments on Structure and Coherence of Paper:

Comments on Grammar, Spelling, etc.:

Appendix C
Plan-for-Revision Sheet

Read carefully all of the comments given by students or the teacher (or both) from the Teacher/Student Comment Sheet. Respond to comments in each category below. Even if comments for a particular category are generally favorable, you still should have something to say concerning improvement, however slight, about that category.

Reconsideration of My Thesis:

Reconsideration of Arguments on Behalf of My Thesis:

Reconsideration of My Use of Text(s):

Reconsideration of the Structure and Coherence of My Paper:

Reconsideration of Grammar, Spelling, etc.:

Sources Cited

Abelard, Peter, *The Story of My Misfortune*, trans. Henry Adam Bellows (New York: Macmillan, 1972).

Addelson, Kathryn Pyne, "Equality and Competition: Can Sports Make a Women of a Girl?" *Women, Philosophy, and Sport: A Collection of New Essays* (Metuchen, NJ: The Scarecrow Press, Inc., 1983), 133-161.

Aristotle, *Nicomachean Ethics,* second edition, trans. Terrence Irwin (Indianapolis: Hackett Publishing Company, Inc., 1999).

Aristotle, *On the Heavens*, trans. W.K.C. Guthrie (Cambridge: Harvard University Press, 1986).

Aristotle, *Politics,* trans. C.D.C. Reeve (Indianapolis: Hackett Publishing Company, Inc., 1998).

Brzezinski, Zbigniew, The Grand Failure: The Birth and Death of Communism in the Twentieth Century (New York: Scribner, 1989).

Camus, Albert, *The Fall* (New York: Knopf, 1957).

Carter, Jimmy, "Just War—or a Just War?" *The New York Times*, March 9, 2003

Darwin, Charles, *Origin of Species* (Washington Square, NY: New York University Press, 1988).

Descartes, Rene, *Meditations on First Philosophy,* trans. Donald A. Cress, third edition (Hackett Publishing Company, Inc., 1993).

Dewey, John, *Experience and Education* (New York: Simon & Shuster, 1997).

Dewey, John, *How We Think* (Mineola, NY: Dover Publications, Inc., 1997).

Diogenes Laertius, *Lives, Vol. II,* trans. R. D. Hicks (Cambridge: Harvard University Press, 1991).

Epicurus, *Principle Doctrines* in *The Epicurus Reader,* ed. Brad Inwood and L. P. Gerson (Indianapolis: Hackett Publishing Company, Inc., 1994).

Freud, Sigmund, "Reflections upon War and Death," *Character and Culture*, ed. Philip Rieff (New York: Macmillan Publishing Company, 1963).

Freud, Sigmund and Wilhelm Fliess, *The Complete Letters of Sigmund Freud to Wilhelm Fliess, 1887-1904,* trans. Jeffrey Moussaieff Masson (Cambridge, MS: The Belknap Press, 1985).

Gandhi, Mohatma, *Selected Political Writings*, ed. Dennis Dalton (Indianapolis: Hackett Publishing Company, Inc., 1996).

Hippocrates, *On Prognosis*, trans. W.H.S. Jones *Hippocrates*, Vol. II, Loeb Classical Library (Cambridge: Harvard University Press, 1923).

Homer, *Iliad*, trans. Richard Lattimore (The University of Chicago Press, 1961).

James, William, *Pragmatism—A New Name for Some Old Ways of Thinking* (New York: Longmans, Green and co., 1943).

Jefferson, Thomas, "The Letters of Thomas Jefferson: 1743-1826: To Thomas Law Poplar Forest, June 1814," (http://odur.let.rug.nl/~usa/P/tj3/writings/brf/jefl230.htm) 10/3/03.

Jung, C. G., "On the Significance of Number Dreams," *Dreams,* ed. Gerhard Adler (Princeton University Press, 1974).

Kant, Immanuel, *Grounding for the Metaphysics of Morals,* trans. James W. Ellington (Indianapolis: Hackett Publishing Company, Inc., 1993).

Locke, John, *Second Treatise of Government*, ed. Peter Laslett (Cambridge: Cambridge University Press, 1988).

Luke, Carmen and Jennifer Gore, *Feminisms and Critical Pedagogy* (New York: Routledge, 1992).

Malcolm, Norman, *Dreaming* (London: Routledge & Paul, 1964).

Mill, John Stuart, *On Liberty* (New York: Penguin Books, 1985).

Nussbaum, Martha, The Therapy of Desire: Theory and Practice in Hellenistic Ethics (Princeton, NJ: Princeton University Press, 1994).

Pascal, Blaise, *Pensées,* trans. A.J. Krailsheimer (London: Penguin Classics, 1995).

Plato, *Apology* in *Five Dialogues,* trans. G.M.A. Grube (Indianapolis: Hackett Publishing Company, Inc., 1981).

Plato, *Laches,* in *Laches and Charmides*, trans. Rosamond Kent Sprague (Indianapolis: Hackett Publishing Company, Inc., 1992).

Russell, Bertrand, *Conquest of Happiness* (New York: Liveright, 1958).

Russell, Bertrand, *The Wisdom of the West* (Garden City, NY: Doubleday, 1959).

Santayana, George,

Schick, Theodore, Jr. and Lewis Vaughn, *How to Think about Weird Things* (Mountain View, CA: Mayfield Publishing Company, 2010).

Sextus Empiricus, *Selections,* ed. Phillip Hallie (Indianapolis: Hackett Publishing Company, Inc., 1985).

Skinner, B. F., *Science and Human Behavior* (New York: Free Press, 1965).

Sterba, James, *The Triumph of Practice over Theory in Ethics* (New York: Oxford University Press, 2005).

Twain, Mark, *The Diary of Adam and Eve* (Kansas City: Hallmark Cards, Inc., 1975).